GIFTS FROM THE LAND

GIFTS
FROM
THE LAND

by Virginia Whitman

MUHLENBERG PRESS   PHILADELPHIA

Type used in this book: Body, 14 on 21 Fairfield; Display, Graphic and Egmont initials

Paper: Flouradull White

ACKNOWLEDGMENTS

I APPRECIATE the permission that has been granted by *Home Life, Moody Monthly, Nature,* and *The News and Leader* of Springfield, Mo., to adapt or reproduce material which was originally published by them.

Quotations of Scripture are from the King James Version except in a couple of instances where permission was granted by Moody Press, Moody Bible Institute, 820 N. LaSalle St., Chicago 10, Ill., to quote from *The New Testament in the Language of the People* by Charles B. Williams.

I am very grateful to Mr. Don Wooldridge, chief photographer for the Missouri Conservation Commission, and to Mr. Gerald R. Massie, assistant director of the Missouri Division of Resources and Development, for the excellent photographs they have provided. Those on pages x, 44–45, 128–29, 149, 162, and the frontispiece are from Mr. Massie; all the others, including that on the cover, from Mr. Wooldridge.

I am thankful for the inspiration I have received by reading from the works of others, and for any thoughts which may have been borrowed from them.

For many recollections that have been incorporated herein, I am indebted to the daily journals my husband has faithfully kept over a decade.

I dedicate this book to all of my prayer-helpers, including my father, and especially my husband, whose encouragement, loyalty, and co-operation, as well as his prayers, have helped me produce it.

Most of all I am grateful to God for this opportunity to magnify Him. If the life of any reader is blessed by this book, the publisher and author would be encouraged to hear of it.

Virginia Whitman

TABLE OF CONTENTS

While the earth remaineth, seedtime and harvest . . .
and summer and winter . . . shall not cease.

—Genesis 8:22

GIFTS FROM THE LAND

MOST PEOPLE can visit the mountains or the seashore only once a year. There they vacation, relax, possibly even meditate for a week or two, trying to give their batteries a charge that will, for another year, spark life through the depleting pull of its days.

To us is given the privilege of dwelling the year round where we have both mountain and beach. Each day we look out upon a lovely expanse of lake which stretches before us as far as the eye can see to the east and to the south. Though the vista is always the same, each morning there is something different to see. On one day the sun comes up in splendor, a big pot of bright color which overflows and sends a rivulet of yellow gold spilling across the water and into our windows. Or another day the lake is on fire. Wraiths of mist rise smoke-like from its surface which is puckered now and then by the skittering of small fish. At times its placid beauty is patterned with a comet-like design evolving from a boat's prow plying swiftly through liquid silver.

Behind us, to the west and north, is a wreath of hills which are in one season a verdant backdrop to our summer world. At another time they are the icily etched limits of our Christmas card panorama. Thus we live, surrounded with beauty, yet a beauty which teems with life—life that varies in size and intensity from a tiny clinging aphid on the tendril of a pea vine to a big buck deer that bounds out of a thicket and gracefully sails over a pasture fence.

In such an environment not a week passes but that we receive some gift from the land—not material gifts, but the priceless intangibles of challenge, inspiration, encouragement, or understanding.

From the beauties of God's handwork, from the wonders of His creation, from the cycle of life which we behold about us—even from its ruthlessness as well as its co-operations—we draw our gifts. It is this unmarketable but invaluable stockpile of resources which we seek to share with you, hoping that by the division of our dividends from the land, your inventory of faith, hope, courage, and inspiration may be increased.

A BOAT'S PROW PLYING SWIFTLY
THROUGH LIQUID SILVER . . .

WINTER

WINTER

ONCE IN a while a heavy snow or ice storm locks us in. We see no one. Because telephone service is not available in our remote area, we hear no human voice except those we share with the public on radio or television. So we are pocketed for a time with only God, each other, and the wild life for companionship.

Nevertheless we feel compensated beyond measure on these occasions by the extra beauty bonus that accompanies the storm. Whichever way we gaze, we behold glory. It sparks such an exhilaration within us that we are in danger, we feel, of internal combustion. Try to picture what we see.

The rolling white expanse of yard is punctured here and there by little dimples in the snow made by hopping wild life. The oak trees are ribboned with ermine and the cedar trees are caped in it. On every stump is a mound of snow, depressed at the center, giving the appearance of a huge raised doughnut generously glazed with frosting. From poles to buildings run strands of macaroni, with electric lines at their core. The shop, feedhouse, and other small buildings resemble frosted loaf cakes. The boat dock and its approach are spread with cottage cheese and surrounded with the skim milk of ice over the cove.

The wire fences have become works of art. The one with the large square meshes is a lattice of crystal, while the chicken wire becomes a filigree of lace. The grape trellis needs only a treble clef to make it a staff from which the notes of "Winter Wonderland" can be wafted by the slight breeze that blows. It sways the trees, and lumps of snow plop to the ground, or a powdery little blizzard of ice particles flurries the air.

Gorgeous cardinals and bluejays take advantage of the setting to practice their modeling. With their vivid feathers fluffed out, they sit on pearl-plated branches, as if

2

hoping to catch the glance of a greeting-card scout who will report their eye appeal to a company artist. A little white-breasted nuthatch plays the show-off as he walks downside-up on the undersides of branches. The glamour birds are unimpressed by his daredevil exhibition.

On the ground, beneath their notice, the smaller birds practice their toe-painting, leaving modernistic designs on the parchment of snow. A fat, jubilant little wren, mounted on a fence post, lets out a merry chortle, advertising to the world that his zest for life is undiminished by the rigors of winter.

We look past the birds to the lacery of interwoven tree branches. Some of them arch clear to the ground with their weight of dazzle. All the shrubs bend in arcs, forming fairy booths. The less airy ones become havens for the birds. Across the arm of the lake the landscape resembles a powdered wig. Along the shoreline the weeds arch like plumes on the flank of an ostrich. There are dapples in the snow along our edge of the lake where a soft-footed doe has made its way to the water to drink, for the lake, being deeper at this point, is not frozen over.

While we have been watching the outdoor scene, the icicles have grown longer, a drop at a time, as roof-warmed snow has melted and dripped from the eaves of the house. At first they were mere stubble of a night's growth of whiskers, but by day's end they are the long white beard of a Santa Claus.

The brief sun of midday drops behind the hill leaving predusk shadows over the panorama. All the wild folk have sought shelter. There is that hush and stillness peculiar to a snow-wrapped area.

We turn from the windows with a sigh. Our "Diorama of Winter" has ended. Tomorrow the beauty will melt and ooze away. The magic spell will be broken as communication with the "outside" is re-established. But we shall be richer because of having been sealed up for a time in our own "Little America."

JANUARY

THIS IS perhaps the least exciting month of our year, yet it has its advantages along with its disadvantages. It is a time when we can stay home more justifiably than at any other time. Nor do we have to keep on our toes lest someone come and find us untidy or unprepared. Only the closest neighbors or hardiest souls seek us out in our hideaway during this frigid season. Of course the outdoor chores must still be done, often under rigorous and unpleasant conditions that are not without hazard.

On the pleasanter side is bird-watching. We have two feeder trays, one at a north window sill and one a few feet farther off, but within view of the same window. We can sit at the kitchen table and stare at the feathered folk while they eat, without batting an eye at what Emily Post might say of such behavior. Our flowers, if there are any, are in the greenhouse window, as we call the glass bay off the kitchen.

The long evenings are filled with game playing, television viewing, or picking black walnut kernels from burglar-proof safes which only the squirrels can crack. Then, if ever, we get caught up on the magazine stack, reading it down to current issues. And of course, as in any month, the days end as they began, with reading the Book.

Though the month may be less exciting than others, at the same time it may be more relaxing, even more profitable. And like the double-faced god for which it was named, we can look two ways: back on the memories of the year just past, rejoicing in God's blessing and bounty, and forward to the ensuing year, anticipating the pleasures and privileges He is sure to provide. And we can listen for His messages, the hidden significance attached to each day's experiences.

SULLIED SNOW

IT IS snowing, bringing beauty by the centimeter, countless "jillions" of flakes ranging from one hundredth to half an inch in size. Emerging from the house to go for the mail, we find the outdoors robed in charcoal gray marked with coin dots of white.

The trip to the mailbox is over a private road, so we meet no other vehicle. We travel our twisting, snow-shrouded lane in silent solitude. To the right and left, weed stalks have become as lovely as a queen fairy's wand. The cedars, humped by the weight of the white crystals, are hostels for the birds. Yet no slightest wing movement shatters the tranquillity of the exquisite scene that unwinds before us. All is serenity and purity until the car's wheels apply the first sully to the white scroll laid out from heaven.

Spiritually, man has debased the image in which God created him, and has become defaced by sin. But as the prophet declared, because of Christ's atonement, those who believe in Him are again made perfect in the beloved, even as the continuing fall of new snow will surely—and soon—blot out the unsightly tracks. "Saith the Lord: though your sins be as scarlet, they shall be as white as snow; though they be red like crimson, they shall be as wool" (Isa. 1:18).

TO THINK ABOUT: *Have I sorrowed over my sullied life and longed for it to be made clean again?*

TO PRAY ABOUT: *Lord, help me to accept Your provision for my purification.*

CIRCLE OF SECURITY

ONE DAY when the ground was covered with snow, and more was still falling, I looked across the cove in time to see a covey of quail silhouetted against the white hillside of the opposite shore. I reached for the binoculars and through the glasses followed their movements. They all scampered into an area beneath a small cedar tree. There the ground was free of snow and fairly dry. The lower overhanging boughs of the evergreen spread an "umbrella" which protected the little birds from some of the wind and cold. There at its base they formed a circle, heads turned outward to detect any approaching danger. Whichever saw it first would sound an alarm whereupon there would be an explosion of air as all took to whirring wings.

Quails instinctively form this circle of security and maintain this unity of watchfulness and mutual concern. God exhorts His people to do likewise. "There should be no schism in the body; but . . . the members should have the same care one for another" (I Cor. 12:25). "Having the same love, being of one accord, of one mind. . . . Look not every man on his own things, but every man also on the things of others" (Phil. 2:2, 4).

Every local church should consist of such a cordon of Christians covenanted together to watch out for one another's welfare. How different our congregations would be, and our communities too, were this so!

TO THINK ABOUT: *Am I a watchful member of my local "covey" of Christians?*

TO PRAY ABOUT: *Lord, help me to be as alert to the forces that endanger my fellow-Christians as I am to those which jeopardize me.*

WEIGHTY SNOWFLAKES

I SLIPPED INTO an old coat and sallied out to the bird feeder. As I placed food on it, I noticed several snowflakes saunter down and park on my coat sleeve. As I studied their lacy beauty, I wondered how fragile particles like that could cave in roofs the way I had read in the newspaper.

Of course it was the combined weight of millions of them that did it. But just how many flakes swung the balance between safety and disaster? Could one tiny flake be the additional weight that caused a mighty roof to collapse? How many fewer flakes would have left the roof intact?

Just one word can cave in the spirit of a fellow creature. I have seen it happen. A single word of reproof can reduce a child to tears. Newspaper reports verify that an adult can be harried into homicide by the scorn or venom packed into one word. That being true, dare I ever be the one to speak a word which would cause such a collapse?

On the other hand, a cheery "Hello!" or a hearty "Fine!" is the word that can salvage a neighbor from despair, or encourage a child to keep trying. For just as God meant for the snow to water the earth and refresh it, so He intends for our words to strengthen those to whom we speak. "A word spoken in due season, how good is it!" (Prov. 15:23).

TO THINK ABOUT: *Have I collapsed my fellow creature's spirit today with ill-advised words?*

TO PRAY ABOUT: *Lord, help me to use words which will strengthen others.*

SEED CATALOGS

ADVERTISING THAT comes in the mail at this time of year indicates that seedsmen are clever salesmen. They use a psychological approach. Just when our eyes may be winter-weary and anxious to see tokens of spring, they are bombarded with brightly colored reproductions of beautiful flowers and luscious fruits. Challenged by the possibilities of such products from our efforts, we get out an order for endless varieties of seeds. We may never get ground broken for all we have ordered, the weeds or blight may take what we do sow, hot winds may dry it up. But discounting all these possibilities, we eagerly pore over the pages to make our selections.

The Bible is a seed catalog too. It contains bright promises of what may be expected from the sown Word. There should be new creations in Christ Jesus: "If any man be in Christ, he is a new creature" (II Cor. 5:17a). We should see growth in Christian character: "Grow in grace, and in the knowledge of our Lord and Saviour Jesus Christ" (II Pet. 3:18). It is an interesting experiment to try to imagine what one would be like if he fulfilled God's expectations.

To THINK ABOUT: *How does God picture the "blossom" and "fruit" that I am to become?*

To PRAY ABOUT: *Lord, help me to fulfil Your pattern.*

CHANGING ICE

A SPELL OF weather which kept the lake frozen over near here gave me a new impression. Heretofore, I had just thought of ice as ice. Now I was interested to observe how much it varied from day to day. At first it seemed merely a smooth, leaden expanse. Then came wind, and it developed streaks all over, as if a throng of skaters had left it covered with blade marks.

Another day it looked like glass on which something had been dropped here and there, leaving shatter spots of crooked cracks radiating from a central point. Then after a partial thaw it developed stream-like swirls resembling an eddying river, only they were ice, not water. Later, various-sized rings appeared, due perhaps to subsurface springs or currents. Ice may be ice, I thought, but it can certainly appear in many patterns.

In Job 6:15–17 ice is compared to deceitful friends. "What time they wax warm, they vanish: when it is hot, they are consumed out of their place."

I wondered if I, in my fellowships, brought reproach on my Lord at any time by being the melting-ice type of friend. Or had I rather stood firm, an illustration to the world of that scriptural friend that "sticketh closer than a brother" (Prov. 18:24).

To THINK ABOUT: *Is my friendship the kind that disappears like ice when trial or misunderstanding arises?*

To PRAY ABOUT: *Lord, help me to be a solid friend.*

THE COVERING

E ARE always interested in the way our domestic bunnies prepare for a "blessed event." They hollow out a spot in some of the lespedeza that is placed in their pens for them to eat. Then they line it with their own fur. When their wee babies arrive, they again pluck fur from their own breasts and completely cover them with it. This keeps the naked little ones warm even in midwinter. You can't see the tiny fellows, but you know they're there by the way the down coverlet rises and falls with their breathing.

God "plucked the covering" for sinful man from His own bosom: "The only begotten Son, which is in the bosom of the Father, he hath declared him" (John 1:18). He sent Christ to shed His blood to cover our sins. "Herein is love, not that we loved God, but that he loved us, and sent his Son to be the propitiation for our sins" (I John 4:10).

All the little rabbits have to do to get the benefit of the covering their mama provides is to nestle there under it. All we have to do is accept in faith God's gracious cover for our unrighteousness.

To THINK ABOUT: *Have I fully appreciated the fact that God expresses His love for us in such a manner?*

To PRAY ABOUT: *Lord, help me gratefully to accept Your cover for my spiritual nakedness.*

DRINKING BIRDS

A COMMON SIGHT, particularly in the morning, is of the birds fluttering down to the lake shore for a drink. There is the brilliant flash of the cock cardinal as he wings down to a brush pile by the water's edge. Then I see the black of a junco's back or the white of its breast, and the vivid coming and going of the bluejays.

It seems an absurd thing to say that birds all know enough to go and get a drink of water—absurd too, but true, is the fact that not all humans are that smart.

"Ho every one that thirsteth, come ye to the waters" (Isa. 55:1). "The Spirit and the bride say, Come. And whosoever will, let him take the water of life freely" (Rev. 22:17).

Despite these cordial invitations, and despite unsatisfied thirsts, many do not come. That is why I say the birds are smarter than humans. They don't try other things first, and then turn to water as a last resort. With no attempt at substitution and no procrastination, birds go to the water and drink freely.

To THINK ABOUT: *Have I been trying substitutes all day long instead of letting my spirit drink from God's well?*

To PRAY ABOUT: *Lord, give me the simple wisdom to drink gladly and gratefully each day, there where alone my soul's thirst can be quenched.*

A GOOD MANY 'POSSUM CHRISTIANS
PROWL OUR CHURCHES

THE PROWLER

IT WAS the kind of night when you're reluctant to leave the warmth of indoors. The moon may be beautiful, but it's a cold beauty. The stars may be twinkling, but that won't prevent ears and nose tips from tingling in the frosty air.

Tigie, however, kept barking so persistently and the guineas cackled so distressfully that we concluded there must be an unwelcome visitor in the hen house. And there was! Investigation revealed a prowling 'possum.

Once the gate was opened, Tigie rushed in and grabbed the old fellow, shaking him into insensibility, or so it seemed. Actually, he was by no means incapacitated until a sharp axe put an end to his pretense.

There are a good many 'possum Christians prowling our churches. They give the appearance of being what they are not. Some people call that hypocrisy, the root meaning of which is "to act a part." Whatever its name, it hinders the Lord's cause.

Christ denounced 'possum Christians in words such as these: "Woe unto you, scribes and Pharisees, hypocrites! for ye devour widows' houses, and for a pretense make long prayer: . . . ye are like unto whited sepulchres, which indeed appear beautiful outward, but are within full of dead men's bones, and of all uncleanness. Even so ye also outwardly appear righteous unto men, but within ye are full of hypocrisy and iniquity" (Matt. 23:14, 27–28).

To THINK ABOUT: *In which areas of my life am I guilty of 'possum practices?*

To PRAY ABOUT: *Lord, make me not simply to appear, but actually to be, a true Christian—fully equipped with that genuine righteousness which does not "act a part" because it does not need to.*

HAWK'S PREY

WE GREATLY enjoy watching fleets of American mergansers, a species of duck, sporting in the water. Down an open channel of the lake will come a flotilla of them, each white breast gleaming like the prow of a ship on her maiden voyage. A tousle-headed female upends in a sudden dive, and the rest follow suit as if by secret signal. After a time she emerges with a shining little silver fish held fast in her deckle-edged beak. The drakes celebrate her success by standing on tiptoe and flapping their wings. A passing gull dips his wing in salute, then circles and stoops to kiss a pretty little wavelet. Again the mergansers dive, nearly simultaneously.

One day as we were spectators of their antics, we saw a large hawk flying over them. They dived. He continued to hover over a particular spot, and as one beautiful, two-foot-long fowl came to the surface, the hawk swooped and lifted it bodily from the water. His prey was as large as he, but was helpless in his clutch, and the brown bird soon winged out of sight, carrying his booty. In his wake the circling waves seemed to spread out in all directions, speeding the message to distant shores: "Blessed be the Lord, who hath not given us a prey to their teeth. Our soul is escaped as a bird out of the snare of the fowlers. . . . Our help is in the name of the Lord" (Ps. 124:6–8).

Satan, our archenemy, daily sets snares to entangle us in our Christian walk. We dare not underestimate his cunning. Only through Christ can we escape being captured by him.

To THINK ABOUT: *Have I realized that apart from God I am as helpless as a duck in the clutches of the enemy?*

To PRAY ABOUT: *Lord, help me to live so close to You that the wicked one can have no power over me.*

WATERING THE CATTLE

WHEN THE temperature remains low for a protracted period, the coves all freeze over. Then comes the difficulty of keeping water open so the cattle can drink. At least once daily, it requires a long walk to where the cattle habitually drink. The ice has to be broken with a heavy sledge hammer. This is strenuous labor. One breathes harder and deeper and the cold seems to penetrate clear down into the lungs. The shore is not even at that point, which makes it hard to retain firm footing. Some times the level of the lake is lower each day, due to readjustment of locks at the dam. Then our chore is even more complicated because ice must be broken under which there is no water before one gets to ice, also to be broken, under which there is water. But how eagerly the cattle drink, once they have access to the water!

Christ in his own body bore the blows which opened for us a way to the water of life, as was prophesied: "In that day there shall be a fountain opened to the house of David and to the inhabitants of Jerusalem for sin and for uncleanness" (Zech. 13:1). Christ Himself testified: "The water that I shall give him shall be in him a well of water springing up into everlasting life" (John 4:14).

To THINK ABOUT: *Have I stood at Calvary and witnessed what it cost Christ to assure me everlasting life?*

To PRAY ABOUT: *Lord, I thank You that through faith alone, without labor or suffering on my part, I can partake of the living water.*

FEBRUARY

THE TEMPO of living advances a little in February. It is a period of getting ready for the bustle of spring when the dormancy of winter is definitely past. On clement days there is outdoor work: cold frames to be renovated, fences to be mended, boats to be repaired. The men take time out to plant crappie beds to insure good fishing for next summer. They hew down a cedar tree, drag it to a likely spot, wire it with rocks, and then sink it.

The pastures are always porcupined with sprouts to be cut; their roots have to be poisoned to prevent a second growth. This is the time for resowing with lespedeza or timothy, and for applications of lime or fertilizer. There are eroded places to be terraced and washouts to be filled with dead timber after it has been sawn down. Fruit trees must be planted to replace those that have died or been broken. They will require mulching and fertilizing.

All the old litter needs to be carried from the chicken house, nests and roosts sprayed, walls whitewashed, and new dry litter put in. A maternity-minded hen or two may be set. Some years we get baby chicks this early. They come by mail on a specified date, and we must be at the box to receive then when Uncle Sam's carrier arrives in late afternoon. They're noisy little rascals, yeeping, no doubt, about their close quarters, a bumpy ride, or a trodden toe. It is surprising, though, how soon heat, feed, and water quiet them down to dozing little fuzz-balls with tiny, fat tummies almost too heavy for one pair of spindly legs to support. There may also be a wobble-legged calf or two, at first a small pile of damp fur, but surprisingly soon a cavorting dynamo, tail held as erect as any antenna, and equally capable of catching the vibrations of approaching spring.

Beginning with the first robin, there is the annual roll call of returning birds as they arrive from wintering south. Inside, the hyacinths and paper-white narcissus come into bloom. Outside, by the last of the month, gay little crocuses are pushing through the bare brown earth. If it is an early season, shy violets may be discovered out in the woods, peeping through when the layers of brown leaves are pulled aside.

The days are getting longer, but at evening there is still the thumbing of growing guides and discussion as to how many hollow stumps to plant with tomatoes (a favorite trick of the gardener because it takes them up off the ground and onto a handy working level where they can be easily staked). There is the perennial plotting to outwit the weeds despite the fact that there has never been a year when they didn't outwit the gardener.

And God is still the Silent Partner, the One without whom there will be neither crops nor creatures. So we still listen for His daily whispers and meditate on them.

CANNIBAL CHICKS

THE CARE of our hundred little chicks has been complicated by a bad practice some of them have developed. In poultry journals it is called cannibalism, because they peck at one another as if they were food. Since they are being fed rations which supposedly contain all the needed nutrients, we can't attribute the undesirable habit to dietary deficiency. We're going to try larger housing facilities and see if that helps.

Cannibalism, however, isn't limited to chickens or uncivilized tribesmen. It has been a common practice among Christians ever since Paul's time: "But if ye bite and devour one another, take heed that ye be not consumed one of another" (Gal. 5:15).

Every time we criticize or gossip about a fellow Christian, we are pecking at him as the little chickens peck at one another. Whenever we discourage him, or rob him of his joy, we are taking a bite out of him. In whatever way we attack him or discomfit him we are being cannibal Christians, operating on just as low a plane as cannibal chickens.

To THINK ABOUT: *Who are the victims of my cannibalism?*

To PRAY ABOUT: *Lord, help me to develop instead of devour my fellow Christians.*

FOGGY HIGHWAYS

On sunday when we left for church services in town, it was clear here on the lake, yet when we got down the road a few miles, we encountered dense fog. It shortened the span of visibility as truly as if a curtain had been hung just in front of the car. This made the driving hazardous. The headlights of approaching cars, turned on for safety's sake even though it was daylight, became visible before the outlines of the cars themselves.

While I was praying for God's care of us, I thought of how often the fogs of uncertainty, sorrow, and fright close down on us in everyday living; and how wonderful it is, when that happens, to have the light of God's Word to help us distinguish the shape of things to come. "Thine ears shall hear a word behind thee, saying, this is the way, walk ye in it" (Isa. 30:21).

Soon we were out of the fog. Once again we could see a normal distance and could accelerate to usual driving speeds. We thanked God that we would arrive safely at His house where we could serve and worship with his people.

To think about: *Am I listening for God's voice to guide me through the fogs that fall on my daily journey?*

To pray about: *Lord, help me to move by the light of Your Word when the way is dim or danger-fraught.*

SELF-MULTIPLYING POSIES

SPRING'S EARLY flowers, the crocuses, are a delight to our eyes now. The yellow ones always come first, lifting their golden chalices to be filled with sunshine. A bit later come the purple ones, royal indeed. We are surprised to note clumps of blossoms where none had appeared in previous years. We suppose that means that the original ones have fruited, and that seed from them has been scattered, and in time produced the others. What a pleasing bonus!

Do we give God that type of pleasure—the joy of seeing other Christians spring up because we have been fruitful, and they have been the product of our fruit-bearing? There are plenty of seed possibilities: "The fruit of the spirit is love, joy, peace, longsuffering, gentleness, goodness, faith, meekness, temperance" (Gal. 5:22–23).

Bear the fruit of love among your neighbors and it will take root in some human heart; and where before there abode no child of God one will then appear. Bear the fruit of long-suffering in that office where the manager is so impatient and inconsiderate, and one day you will discover a Christian there. Bear the fruit of meekness in the midst of a society where each is straining for prestige, and there a Christian will, in time, rear his head.

TO THINK ABOUT: *Who that I know is a Christian because I bore fruit?*

TO PRAY ABOUT: *Lord, help me, as a believer, to bear fruit after my kind.*

AIR CURRENTS

I CAN USUALLY see something interesting while I'm sitting in the car at the mailbox waiting for the delivery. Often I've noticed the action of the wind in the trees. The peculiar feature about it is that not all trees are affected in the same degree. Only a few leaves will be fluttering in a tree to the left, while just across the road the whole top of a tree is swaying violently. I attribute this difference to the topography of the land and consequent difference in air currents.

Wind is a symbol of the Holy Spirit. "The wind bloweth where it listeth, and thou hearest the sound thereof, but canst not tell whence it cometh and whither it goeth: so is every one that is born of the Spirit" (John 3:8). And just as all trees are not moved to the same degree by the same wind blowing through them, so all people do not manifest with equal emotion the presence of the one Holy Spirit. Some weep, while others give little outer evidence of inner feelings.

Emotional demonstration of the Spirit's presence is not essential, but possession of the Spirit is absolutely crucial. He is the One from whom comes all strength, guidance, instruction, comfort, power for victory, skill for achievement, *everything*. "The manifestation of the Spirit is given to every man to profit withal" (I Cor. 12:7). Therefore we should not be satisfied except as we have some personally satisfying token of His abiding in us, whether it be comparable to swaying treetops or only to fluttering leaves. The Spirit must blow upon us, and through us. That is the essential thing.

TO THINK ABOUT: *Does the Spirit of God really dwell in me?*

TO PRAY ABOUT: *Lord, let Your Spirit have access to every area of my life that I may abound in all things.*

TRAVELING BIRDS

BY THE last of the month, if the season is open, we hear the honking of wild geese. Looking up, we see graceful **V** formations winging their way toward northern nesting grounds. A little later we observe occasional flocks of other birds in their migratory excursions, though we are not located on any of the main flyways. As a rare migratory treat we once saw a whistling swan, and a couple of other times pelicans, but these were unusual.

Bird biologists as well as laymen have, from early times, theorized about the acknowledged mystery of migration. How to explain the fact that the young of Pacific golden plovers, born in the northlands of Alaska and Siberia, deserted by parents while still too young to fly great distances, wing their way unchaperoned and unguided two thousand miles to the Hawaiian Islands? Still more mysteriously, the American golden plover, after nesting in northern Alaska or Canada, flies to Labrador and then south to Argentina. Neither ever gets confused and takes the wrong route. They follow unerringly a flyway they have never traveled before.

The answer is most certainly to be found in God "which doeth great things and unsearchable: marvellous things without number" (Job 5:9). The migration of birds is only one of the innumerable evidences in the world of nature that we have a God of all wisdom.

TO THINK ABOUT: *How wonderful to have a God who can equip a bird with a built-in compass.*

TO PRAY ABOUT: *Lord, increase my ability to appreciate Your magnificent creative powers.*

WE SEE GRACEFUL V
FORMATIONS OF WILD GEESE

CURIOUS CAVES

IN OUR county, and in the area generally, there are numerous limestone caves. I have always been disappointed that we have none on our own land. Sometimes when we have guests come from afar, we take them to visit one of these caves. They never fail to marvel at the curious formations and the beautiful hues to be found in them.

While the guides give their learned lectures on the manner of formation, the difference between stalactites and stalagmites, the uniformity of year-round temperature within the caves, and so on, I think about the God who is responsible for it all. "Whatsoever the Lord pleased, that did He in heaven, and in earth, in the seas, and all deep places" (Ps. 135:6).

In the presence of such beautiful crystalline formations one cannot but ascribe praise to God. "Many, O Lord my God, are thy wonderful works which thou hast done.... If I would declare and speak of them, they are more than can be numbered" (Ps. 40:5). It is a striking thought that one cannot go anywhere in the universe but that he will behold the wonders and beauties of God's handiwork.

TO THINK ABOUT: *Have I appreciated the beauty God has embodied in all things from the least to the greatest, from the deepest cave to the highest star?*

TO PRAY ABOUT: *Lord, let the beauty You have created inspire me also to be a creator of loveliness in life.*

THE HIDEAWAY

AT THIS SEASON of the year it is easy to detect which trees are hollow by the holes the woodpeckers have hammered out. There are no concealing leaves. I once saw an amusing drama featuring just such an opening.

It was a crisp but sunshiny day, cold enough to make me move briskly as I walked through the woods. The trees were bare except for the white oaks which always cling to their summer finery long after it has lost its beauty of form and color. The earth was brown, except in sheltered places where now and then I caught a glint of the velvet, emerald pile of moss.

I heard a hubbub in the trees and I discovered a bevy of birds tormenting a blinky-eyed little screech owl cringing on a limb. Suddenly he seemed to muster a spurt of courage, and flying right out from under their noses (or perhaps I should say beaks) he darted into a hole in an adjoining hollow tree. Within this refuge I could see his head silhouetted against the opening. The other birds flew back and forth in front of it, screaming and scolding, but the little owl was unperturbed, confident that his refuge was secure.

The believer too is in a secure situation. "Your life is hid with Christ in God" (Col. 3:3). The psalmist confesses: "Thou are my hiding place; thou shalt preserve me from trouble" (Ps. 32:7).

To THINK ABOUT: *Amid the outcry and assaults of the world, where have I been seeking refuge and security?*

To PRAY ABOUT: *Lord, increase my faith that in all circumstances I may have utter confidence in You.*

MARCH

THIS IS the month when nature and farmer both get into gear. If weather is favorable, buildings are painted, the garden is plowed, spray is applied to the fruit trees. Planting traditionally begins with potatoes on St. Patrick's Day, followed by lettuce, radishes, and both garden and sweet peas. Tomatoes and some flowers will already have been started in cold frames or flats. Strawberry, rhubarb, and cabbage plants must be set out.

It's a busy time with poultry: little chickens, ducks, or goslings; the guineas come later. The tame rabbits of course run a year-round factory. The pert little wrens have officiously pre-empted several locations for nest sites: back of the pitchfork in the barn (which necessitates our taking another down there to use until hatching is over), an old box in the garage, a tackle section of the boat dock, and even an old bucket up-ended over a fence post by the shop door.

Friendly little coots paddle around the dock and may even be inveigled into coming ashore and plucking worms from the gardener's hand. Fishing for crappie starts again and we begin to see Wilson's snipes. The swallows resume housekeeping in the chimneys and e'er long we hear the shrill, fretful cheep-cheep of the always-hungry young.

Fire danger reaches a peak because of the seasonal winds and because this is the time of year when those who will not be convinced of better conservation practices start burning off their land in preparation for replanting. The fire generally escapes them and spreads to the adjoining fields and woodlands of other residents who decry the damage to forests and wild life.

Paradoxically, a late blizzard sweeps through the state on a farewell tour, and finds its snowflakes rivaled by the falling petals of service berry and wild plum blossoms. The dwarf iris are edging the flower beds with purple while the forsythias complement their color with their golden bells. The narcissus trim the yard with yellow and white frills. Buds begin to swell on tulips and lilacs.

Dusk comes later each day. Bedtime, however, is moved up, because weary bones and aching muscles demand it. Nevertheless, sleep does not come so quickly but that there is opportunity to inventory and re-evaluate the day's activities in spiritual terms.

SPRING PLOWING

HE BUDS on the trees and shrubs are swelling and showing green tips. The air is balmy, and the breezes no longer blustery. The birds have begun their courting serenades, and spring flowers are commencing to dot the landscape. All of that spells time to plow, and many a furrow is being turned to ready the ground for the sowing of crops.

Every glimpse of fresh-turned sod is a reminder of the prophet's call: "Break up your fallow ground; for it is time to seek the Lord, till he come and rain righteousness upon you" (Hos. 10:12).

We all have unplanted areas in our hearts which we need to ready for cultivation. They need to be planted through Bible study: "The seed is the word of God" (Luke 8:11). Through this planting they may produce righteousness. Some of us need those undeveloped areas sown with Scripture about giving and tithing so that righteousness in finances will flourish. Others need texts to be sown on evangelism so that righteousness manifested in soul-winning will be the product. Still others need texts to be planted on faith, so that victory in daily living will result.

To THINK ABOUT: *Which area of my heart is fallow and needs to be broken up and sown with God's seed?*

To PRAY ABOUT: *Lord, stir me to diligence in studying Your Word.*

INDIAN RELICS

Every time we plow a certain area on our farm, we turn up more spearheads. So many have been collected from this one spot that we suspect it may have been a place where the Indians made them. The idea is borne out by the fact that many stone chips are found that seem to have been started and then discarded because they were found to be unsatisfactory for some reason.

I am not sure what kind of stone they are. It is not flint. The edges indicate they were chipped into shape. Considering the fact that they were handmade with the crudest of tools, I suppose it is remarkable that they are as well crafted as they are. But to us who are accustomed to the precision of machine-made articles, they look very imperfect. The two sides are never identical, for one is invariably a trifle longer or wider than the other. Nevertheless, they served the purpose for which they were intended, as weapons to aid the battling redskin.

How many of God's people are trying to arm themselves with spears of their own making? With these they propose to win the battle of life instead of looking to God who said, "Not by might, nor by power, but by my spirit, saith the Lord of hosts" (Zech. 4:6). "This assembly shall know that the Lord saveth not with sword and spear: for the battle is the Lord's" (I Sam. 17:47).

To THINK ABOUT: *What kind of spearheads am I trying to forge to assure success in the battle of life?*

To PRAY ABOUT: *Lord, help me to depend for victory on Your Holy Spirit alone.*

FIRE IN THE FOREST

WE HAVE been plagued by forest fires. Each time the state conservation department has co-operated splendidly in sending out a crew of forestry men to fight the fire. Until they arrive, however, we ourselves have to jump in and fight lest the blaze get out of bounds and destroy our timber, cattle guards, fences, or buildings.

The other day, though knowing of no fire, we made a routine check and found a fire burning its way rapidly toward our property. With fire rake we quickly tried to sweep fallen leaves from its path and prevent its spread. There was no time to go for help though it was desperately needed. We could only pray for it. The smoke was blinding to the eyes and searing to the lungs. The heat was painful and the exercise exhausting. Just as we were in danger of being surrounded by the flames, a fire fighting crew pulled in and took over.

After a backfire had been set and the blaze brought under control, they told us, "One of the conservation planes spotted the fire from the air, and saw you battling it. They radioed us to get over here quick, that your situation was critical." We thanked God for His providence.

Just as the plane pilot looked down from above, discerned our need, and dispatched men to our rescue, so God from His heaven beholds our difficulties and delegates individuals and resources to our aid. "The Lord is thy keeper . . . the Lord shall preserve thy going out and coming in . . . even for evermore" (Ps. 121:5, 8).

To THINK ABOUT: *Have I realized that God's eye is ever upon me, not primarily for detection of misconduct, but for protection from misfortune?*

To PRAY ABOUT: *Lord, help me to appreciate and trust in Your loving, watchful care.*

34

FLOWERS THAT FADE

WENT FOR a walk to enjoy the springtime bursting out all over. I saw the beet red of the sorrel's first leaves crowding through rocky crevices; the damp, greening ground, polka-dotted with the blue of fallen cedarberries; the tiny green stars of moss lichen, not much bigger than the asterisk of a typewriter keyboard; the furled umbrella tip of a May-apple leaf, still colorless like flesh, but thrusting aside last year's oak leaves beneath the parent tree; the moist russet of fungi unfolding amidst bits of gray gravel; and the velvety cabbage heads of mullein leaves rosetting the landscape like upholstery buttons on a chair.

Then I picked up a last year's sycamore ball. It disintegrated at my touch into a flurry of antique gold snowflakes. How quickly, I thought, do the blooms fade, make seeds, and disappear. "The grass withereth, and the flower thereof falleth away" (I Pet. 1:24). Beautiful as it is, and to be admired and enjoyed, the flora around me is perishable, and therefore cannot take precedence over that which lasts forever.

"Wherefore, if God so clothe the grass of the field, which today is, and tomorrow is cast into the oven, shall he not much more clothe you, O ye of little faith?" (Matt. 6:30).

To THINK ABOUT: *Am I more concerned about material things than about spiritual ones?*

To PRAY ABOUT: *Lord, help me to distinguish properly the relative values of things temporal and things eternal.*

FROST-NIPPED SPROUTS

WE HAVE had several days of unseasonable warmth lately. It has started some of the flowering bulbs pushing a rosette of green leaves through the moist, dark earth. Fearing that a hard and killing frost would yet come, I gathered leaves and spread them over those rash and tender little sprouts, as a mother pulls the covers back over a small, active child who has kicked them off.

Babes in Christ, newly born into His kingdom, are sometimes overeager in their new experience too. With commendable zeal they push out into the cold world, anxious to bloom for Christ and shed abroad His fragrance, only to be rudely met with icy indifference, or scoffing and ridicule. Like tender shoots shocked by a chilling frost, they are nipped back, their enthusiasm killed.

Just as the frost-blackened plant must make new growth, so the babe in Christ must make new spiritual growth after such a setback. Sometimes his experience has been such a blow to him that he is stunted and does not easily repeat his first thrust of growth. Have we more mature Christians been at fault in not anticipating his backset and protecting him against it?

Christ's command lays upon us just such a responsibility: "Support the weak" (I Thess. 5:14), and "We then that are strong ought to bear the infirmities of the weak, and not to please ourselves" (Rom. 15:1).

To THINK ABOUT: *Am I seeking to protect fellow-Christians from some of life's damaging experiences?*

To PRAY ABOUT: *Lord, when I am nipped by someone's coldness or hostility, help me, in spite of it, to show new growth immediately.*

PLANTING POTATOES

THIS WAS potato-planting day and it was my job to cut up the seed potatoes. The instructions were to have a sizable chunk of potato with every eye, and yet to get as many such chunks as possible from each potato. That made it kind of like a game, a challenge to my skill. On some of the potatoes it seemed as if the eyes were all in one end, defying me to visualize a way of separating them and yet have sufficient vegetable matter with each eye.

The human eye is a wonderful mechanism. Scientists call it the most sensitive light detector in existence. Though a camera corresponds to it remarkably well, man has never been able to design as completely efficient and flexible an instrument as God did.

I heard of a child once who had been so indoctrinated with the truth of Job 34:21, "His eyes are upon the ways of man, and he seeth all his goings," that the passage created fear and resentment in him. In later life it proved actually to be a hindrance to spiritual development, until he learned how to interpret it properly. "Beloved," he heard a speaker explain, "what this passage points out is that God loves you so much He can't take His eyes off of you. 'The eyes of the Lord run to and fro throughout the whole earth, to shew himself strong on the behalf of them whose heart is perfect toward him' " (II Chron. 16:9). After that it became a source of comfort rather than of anxiety to know that God's eyes were always upon him.

To THINK ABOUT: *Are there times when I would rather get out of God's sight than be under His constant surveillance?*

To PRAY ABOUT: *Lord, make perfect my heart that I may never be embarrassed or unwilling, but grateful, to have Your eyes of love look upon me.*

38

POINT OF VIEW

THE LAKE was "steaming" in the first sunlight of the day as we drove out on a recent morning. You could tell where the areas of water interlaced with the land among the hills by the wraiths of vapor rising from them. It resembled the froths of spun sugar candy offered for sale at county fairs.

Nature's newly green spring robe was studded with silver sequins of dew. Here and there on the hillsides were little white gauze-like patches which were spangled with drops that glittered like rhinestones when the sun's first rays struck them. To me they looked like jeweled bits of veiling; to another they might have been only spider webs.

Isn't that the way with a good bit of life? One man's treasure is another man's trash. Viewpoint determines which; it determines whether something intrigues or irritates, whether it is a matter for pessimism or optimism. The gospel itself may be assessed from divergent viewpoints: "We preach Christ crucified, unto the Jews a stumbling-block, and unto the Greeks foolishness; but unto them which are called, both Jews and Greeks, Christ the power of God, and the wisdom of God" (I Cor. 1:23–24).

With the Lord Jesus Christ as personal Savior, a man has a wholly new viewpoint—on everything. "If any man be in Christ, he is a new creature: old things are passed away; behold, all things are become new" (II Cor. 5:17).

TO THINK ABOUT: *Has my outlook been transformed through Christ?*

TO PRAY ABOUT: *Lord, help me to see everything from Your viewpoint.*

SHELTER AND SHADE

A RECENT VISITOR was captivated by the low green bowl of May-apple blossoms on her dressing table in the guest room. Their petals were so waxy white, around delicate yellow stamens and a fat, pale green pistil, and their fragrance was so intoxicating, that she commented more than once about them.

May apples grow about a foot high. They are found in patches, and can be recognized at some distance because of their parasol leaves atop a handle-like stem. If I were a fairy, I would choose to dwell in a "forest" of May apples. In blossom time it would smell like a perfume factory, and their umbrella leaves would keep out the rain and sun.

However, I have a better dwelling place than a May-apple grove: "He that dwelleth in the secret place of the most High shall abide under the shadow of the Almighty" (Ps. 91:1). "Thou hast been a shelter for me. . . . I will trust in the covert of thy wings" (Ps. 61:3–4).

No other refuge so secure as this is available to mankind. It is surer than storm cellars or bomb shelters. It is eternal.

To THINK ABOUT: *In life's storms am I seeking shelter under something as fragile as a May apple's leaf?*

To PRAY ABOUT: *Lord, help me to dwell in Your secret place, protected by Your presence.*

MILK FED

THE OTHER day Tigie, the dog, brought in a baby rabbit. She had been playing with the little cottontail, but had been careful not to injure it. Knowing it was too small to fend for itself, we put it in a box in the kitchen, named it Buster, and began wet-nursing it.

First we fed it with an eye dropper. Every two or three hours the wiggly four inches of soft fur was picked up and fed milk until its little tummy felt like a foam rubber cushion. As soon as we went in to town we bought a doll's nursing bottle and initiated Buster into its use.

It was fun to see him pull on the nipple, making bubbles in the bottle. His little tongue which darted out to mop up spilled drops was a strawberry pink. Soon he reached the cabbage-leaf-and-carrot stage of diet. Eventually he could be turned loose to fend for himself.

Paul speaks of baby Christians who were not yet beyond the milk stage: "I have fed you with milk, and not with meat: for hitherto ye were not able to bear it, neither yet now are ye able" (I Cor. 3:2). It is written: "For every one that useth milk is unskilful in the word of righteousness: for he is a babe. But strong meat belongeth to them that are of full age, even those who by reason of use have their senses exercised to discern both good and evil" (Heb. 5:13–14).

To THINK ABOUT: *Am I, as a Christian, in the milk or the meat stage?*

To PRAY ABOUT: *Lord, help me to grow spiritually that I may not remain a baby Christian all my life.*

THE WAKE-ROBIN OR TRILLIUM,
SYMBOLIC OF THE TRINITY

TRILLIUM AND SHAMROCK

*A*MONG THE early plants to be found in our woods is the wake-robin or trillium. It is a three-leafed plant with a blossom rising above the trio of mottled green leaves. The bloom has three green, spreading, outer sepals, and three erect, dark, purplish-red petals.

The wood sorrel is another early plant with three-parted leaves which are similar to a clover or shamrock. Greenhouses market them under the name of Oxalis.

Both trillium and wood sorrel are symbolic of the Trinity: three parts, yet a unity.

There is God the Father, infinite source of all that is in me and around me: "O Lord God of hosts, who is a strong Lord like unto thee? or to thy faithfulness round about thee? . . . The heavens are thine, the earth also is thine" (Ps. 89:8, 11).

There is God the Son: " Jesus the author and finisher of our faith; who for the joy that was set before him endured the cross, despising the shame, and is set down at the right hand of the throne of God" (Heb. 12:2).

There is God the Holy Spirit: "Even the Spirit of truth, whom the world cannot receive, because it seeth him not, neither knoweth him: but ye know him; for he dwelleth with you, and shall be in you" (John 14:17).

How wonderful to be related to God the Father through God the Son and to have God the Holy Spirit as royal guest in our household!

To THINK ABOUT: *Are Father, Son, and Holy Spirit equally real to me?*

To PRAY ABOUT: *Lord, help me to rejoice in each member of the Trinity, and in Your perfect Unity.*

SEEDTIME

SEEDTIME

IN THE spring I have purple spots before my eyes. It isn't high blood pressure, it's bird's-foot violets. Wild pansies, some people call them, and sometimes they are almost pansy size. If they're the bicolored ones, the two lower petals are velvety purple, which reminds one of pansies too.

Lovely as they are, they have their competitors. The whole landscape is spattered with pastel tints. Come with me for a walk in the woods and you'll see what I mean.

That mauve blur you see doesn't mean you need to consult an oculist. It's bluets, tiniest of spring flowers, millions of them carpeting the open places. That patch of white over there that looks like frost is a lush growth of dainty rue anemones. And down yonder there where it looks like a blizzard snaggled on the brown tree limbs you'll find wild plums abloom, their fragrance making certain their identity. That lovely veil caught in the branches over to the right isn't a runaway bride's finery. It's a dogwood tree, the virgin-white petals of its flowers bearing a diminutive "rust" stain which legend attributes to the nails that pierced His hands.

In the other direction, the redbud blooms look like strawberry soda splattered against the sky, while at our feet the green turf is held down by brass rivets which are buttercups. That deep purple is the first of the wild larkspur.

Out from under the trees you can see the red-violet of verbenas and the bright orange of puccoons. Down by the spring we can find the heart-shaped leaves of the true violet, the meadow-gold of Johnny-jump-ups, the green of wild bleeding heart's fern-like leaves, and the tall stems of shooting stars, their pink petals turned back as if streamlined for speed.

Or come with me and see the nestful of eggs the cardinals have in the cedar by the garage. Then we'll go peep at the brown thrasher brooding her young in the multi-flora rose hedge by the barn gate. Or would you be interested in the grass cradle that rocks from a branch of the Chinese elm? That is the orchard oriole's nursery. Papa oriole of the shining black head and chestnut waistcoat is flying to and fro so importantly.

Or if you want to see parental pride, come with me down to the boat dock where the bluebirds are trying to fill the bottomless stomachs of their growing children. And we mustn't forget the catbird that homes in the mock orange bush. He gives daily concerts to prove that his grand-opera-voiced kin, the mockingbird, isn't really his superior—much.

What's that you're muttering about food for the eye, but none for the stomach? Well comfort yourself and we'll see what we can do about that. I know a place where the wild strawberries grow, tart yet sweet ruby gems whose flavor exceeds the best of the cultivated ones. And if you wish, we can gather emerald pokeweed greens or lambs-quarter. We can find mushrooms on the way. From the midst of those layers of fallen cedar needles the sponge-like beige tops of the morels pop up. Don't confuse them with the deep red wrinkled folds of the gyromitra which isn't so edible. And aren't those vivid orange caps (*Cantharellis cinnebarius*) gay little things? Look at yonder tiny starlike formations. They're fungi too, as well as those little whitish coral-like stems, also this funny growth that resembles a head of cauliflower.

Tell me, is there any other season that so amply demonstrates the marvelous creative power of God? Our eyes have been filled with the wonder of it, at our feet, to our right and our left, near by and afar. Now look up.

"Lift up your eyes on high, and behold who hath created these things, that bringeth out their host by number: . . . the everlasting God, the Lord, the Creator of the ends of the earth" (Isa. 40:26, 28).

APRIL

This is the month when spring whoops in with a rush. We spend our days vainly trying to keep up with her. Rain, though a needed blessing, sometimes conspires with the wind, and both hinder us. Lacking rain, there is still some danger of fire.

The trees are budding, tinging the landscape with an illusion of green. The Kerria, japonica, and tulips brighten the yard with their gay bloom while lilacs perfume the air. Spears of iris, lily of the valley and day lily have pierced the ground, but so have the weeds! The dahlia and some other bulbs are to be planted, as well as cucumbers, melons, and the like. Winter mulches must be removed, also storm windows taken out and replaced with screens. Fruit trees must be sprayed as soon as the petals have fallen.

At daybreak the wild turkeys gobble, telling their mates to watch as they take off from some tall tree where they've spent the night. A bachelor bobwhite whistles to a passing lady quail, beginning a courtship that culminates in a nestful of eggs in the fence row.

The tree frogs strike up their band at dusk, and from the woodlot comes the first plaintive call of the whippoorwill. (Time now for the women to take over the job of bringing in the wood, the hill folk say.)

Now, at eve, too tired to do anything else, we loiter on the dock or near-by bank, dangling minnows before inquisitive crappie or casting lures where bass are known to lurk. And while we wait for a fish to strike we review the day and let our wonderful, never-changing, ever-provident God speak to us through the events which have transpired.

48

COW CHIP

THE SUN had pried a crack in the eastern horizon and would soon have a hole big enough to climb through. In spite of that, my toes and fingers tingled in the early morning chill as we set out to find the cattle. But the same heavy frost which made the air so crimpy had also put a lovely, feathery coat on every stalk and stick. As the light hit them they sparkled like coronation jewels. Even a lowly cow chip, because it was crusted with frost, took on the appearance of a diamond tiara.

I suppose if you assembled all the leading artists and craftsmen they couldn't tell you how to make a cow chip look pretty. But Almighty God had done it, and without any special research or effort.

God also transforms people. Louise was paying her folks a farewell visit last week before she set sail for Africa to become a missionary nurse. When she spoke in church about the people's needs there and what she hoped to do for them, it seemed as though a light went on inside her. I heard one farmer say, "I used to think Louise was right plain, but she was plumb beautiful when she was talking today."

"They looked unto him and were radiant" (Ps. 34:5, A.S.V.). "Then thou shalt see and be radiant, and thy heart shall thrill" (Isa. 60:5, A.S.V.).

To THINK ABOUT: *How radiantly lovely would I be if God were given unchecked opportunity in my life?*

To PRAY ABOUT: *Lord, help me look to You and permit You to transform me.*

COOING DOVES

MOURNING DOVES are such neat, pretty birds. Their beauty has to be seen to be properly appreciated. The breast is a pinkish-gray and merges into a delicate sky blue on the flanks which are almost hidden by their gray-brown wing coverts. Their eyes are so bright, their feathers so sleek, their feet so trim. But their nests—ah, that's another matter.

I was meandering around the mailbox waiting for the carrier one evening when I spied a dove nest on the lower limb of a large oak. It was a mere handful of sticks, quite flat and so untidily balanced that I wondered what kept the eggs from rolling away or the young from falling out and breaking their necks.

A bird watcher once observed, "If these doves just employed some of the time and ardor they usually put into billing and cooing into trying to construct a safe and substantial home, the result would be a better nest."

Similar criticism is often leveled at Christians. "If they would put as much effort into such and such as they do into their hallelujahs and amens, the result would be so and so." Too often the criticism is justified. "Give none occasion to the adversary to speak reproachfully," Paul exhorted; so live "that the name of God and his doctrine be not blasphemed" (I Tim. 5:14; 6:1). Our practice should tally with our preaching.

To THINK ABOUT: *What deficiencies in my daily living bring reproach on the name of Christ?*

To PRAY ABOUT: *Lord, help me to so conduct all my affairs, private as well as public, that Your doctrine is not dishonored.*

51

RAINBOW OF PROMISE

THE OTHER afternoon I looked across the lake to the two-mile-distant shoreline surmounted by green hills. They were veiled with a haze which I recognized as sheets of heavy rain, evidently falling steadily over there though not in our area. Soon boats came scudding past as if their operators were hastening to keep ahead of the storm. Still the rain did not come.

Instead, the sun came out and there was a beautiful rainbow. One end seemed to rest in the valley between two of yonder rain-shrouded hills. Across the sky was a lovely varicolored span, making a perfect arc. Often before I had seen fragments of rainbow, but rarely the entire arch in all its loveliness, such as I now beheld.

It spoke to me of the promises of God. How encouraged we should be that there is a promise to cover every situation. How challenged we should be to familiarize ourselves with them—and be motivated by them. "Having therefore these promises, dearly beloved, let us cleanse ourselves from all filthiness of the flesh and spirit, perfecting holiness in the fear of God" (II Cor. 7:1). His promises are to be our incentive to cleanliness and purity of heart.

To THINK ABOUT: *Are God's promises for me no more than a bank statement, just an assurance of something to draw upon?*

To PRAY ABOUT: *Lord, may the consideration of Your promises stimulate me to want cleansing and holiness.*

FALLING RAIN

IT WAS raining when we went to bed. I lay for some time listening to the water dripping from the eaves and running from the gutters. It was a welcome sound, for we needed the rain to make things grow.

God says: "As the rain cometh down, and the snow from heaven, and returneth not thither, but watereth the earth and maketh it bring forth and bud, that it may give seed to the sower and bread to the eater: So shall my word be that cometh forth out of my mouth: It shall not return unto me void, but it shall accomplish that which I please, and it shall prosper in the thing whereto I sent it" (Isa. 55:10).

Whenever, by the Spirit's prompting, I give out God's Word, either orally or in print, it will accomplish something He has purposed. Just as I shall not see all the vegetation that results from the rain, so I may not see all that results from the giving out of God's Word. But I can rest assured that it shall prosper in the thing whereto He sent it.

To THINK ABOUT: *Do I give out God's word in faith that there will be results?*

To PRAY ABOUT: *Lord, help me to be faithful in witnessing even though I do not always see what is accomplished by it.*

HUNGRY ORIOLES

I N THE Chinese elm just outside the kitchen window there is a nestful of baby orchard orioles. While I do the dishes I like to watch the mother and father birds coming with insects to feed the little ones. They can bring only one small bug or worm at a time, so feeding their babies becomes a dawn-to-dusk project that permits no slackening on the part of the parents.

The nestlings eagerly hold their gaping mouths wide open to receive the food. No coaxing is needed to get them to eat. No forced feeding is required. Each little oriole is more than anxious to stuff himself with the nourishment offered him.

God's children usually have to be begged and admonished to read God's Word. We want only "teaspoonfuls" at a time, and in effect stick out our tongues when pastors and Bible school teachers offer us more. And then we wonder why we are such weak and powerless Christians.

Paul declared: "Brethren, I commend you to God, and to the word of his grace, which is able to build you up, and to give you an inheritance among all them which are sanctified" (Acts 20:32). Job said, "I have esteemed the words of his mouth more than my necessary food" (Job 23:12).

To THINK ABOUT: *Do I relish food for my body more than I do food for my soul?*

To PRAY ABOUT: *Lord, help me to yearn for a daily feeding on Your Word.*

JEW'S EAR

ONE OF many unusual fungi formations to be discovered by an observant eye is the "Jew's ear." It usually appears on rotting wood, a fallen limb or tree trunk.

One can understand why the word "ear" appears in its name: it is a dark, smoky brown, almost black mushroom, in shape very similar to the human ear. The term "Jew's ear," however, can be accounted for only as evidence of someone's racial prejudice many years ago, a prejudice of which I am regretfully reminded every time I see one of these distinctive fungi.

Gentiles have an unparalleled debt to the Jew: to them we owe our law (derived from the Decalogue), our Bible (written entirely by Jews with but one possible exception), even our Savior (Mary was a Jewish virgin). Besides, there is the command of God to love all our fellow-men of every nationality or race. Finally, there is God's own promise—and the warning implicit in it—made to the great Hebrew patriarch: "I will bless them that bless thee, and curse him that curseth thee" (Gen. 12:3).

In view of all this, how dare we depreciate any Jewish person? Rather we should so yearn for his spiritual need that we, like Paul, could " . . . wish that myself were accursed from Christ" (Rom. 9:1–4) for the sake of their race and its salvation.

TO THINK ABOUT: *Do I love Jews, and all other minority groups, and yearn for their salvation?*

TO PRAY ABOUT: *Lord, root all un-Christlike prejudice out of my heart.*

REJECTED COURTSHIP

*A*MONG THE more frequent patrons of our bird feeders are the "red birds." Early in our bird feeding experience we were disappointed to observe quarrelsome behavior on the part of such handsome creatures. Now we find it also amusing. Many of the cardinals' characteristic actions seem so human.

As spring approaches, courting comes into the picture too. One day we observed a male cardinal light on a branch beside a female. She immediately moved over. He did too. She flew to another branch. He followed her. She moved over again. So did he. After several repetitions of this, she took wing again and lit on a perpendicular stick which had been thrust into the ground the season before as a tomato stake. This time there was no room for him to alight beside her! We laughed at her skilful maneuver. She just didn't want to be wooed!

When the precious Spirit of God comes wooing us earth folks we often act as if we're afraid He might get too close. We believe in being good, but not too good. So we move away from the promised Comforter, the "Paraclete" who would "go alongside" with us. And thus we disobey God: "Grieve not the holy Spirit of God, whereby ye are sealed unto the day of redemption" (Eph. 4:30).

To THINK ABOUT: *Have I resisted the wooing of the Holy Spirit?*

To PRAY ABOUT: *Lord, help me not to grieve or quench but to receive Your Spirit with joy.*

SWOOPING BUZZARDS

THE OTHER day we kept seeing buzzards lighting across the cove to feed on something. Finally our curiosity prompted us to get in the boat and oar over to investigate. What had attracted them was the carcass of a paddlefish.

This scaleless, blue-gray, finny creature has a long paddle-like snout, approximately one-third the length of the body, resembling an oversize duck bill. Its food consists of minute organisms secured by swimming with its mouth open.

It has an interesting habit of leaping clear of the water and falling back with a resounding smack which can be heard for some distance, because the fish attains quite a large size. The one on which the buzzards were feeding had probably weighed about thirty pounds, but by evening it had been picked clean, leaving nothing but the bony skeleton.

How had the paddlefish met death? Apparently it had been caught, probably on a trotline, and then had been "staked out" in the lake like a cow in pasture, by tying a small rope around its snout. Evidently it had managed to break its tether and swim away, for the cord was trailing, but it was still knotted around the snout, making it impossible for the creature to feed.

Not only paddlefish get bound with cords. It has been said that while the Bible keeps one from sin it is also true that sin keeps one from the Bible. "His own iniquities shall take the wicked himself, and he shall be holden with the cords of his sins. He shall die without instruction" (Prov. 5:22-23).

To THINK ABOUT: *What sin is binding me?*

To PRAY ABOUT: *Lord, grant that I be not destroyed by my neglect of Your Word.*

SCAMPERING SQUIRREL

TIGIE TREED a squirrel in an oak by the garage the other day. Clawing at the trunk as if she might ascend it any second, she had the little rodent so frightened he climbed to one of the tiptop limbs of the tree. There being no adjoining tree to which he could jump, he leaped off into space, landing on a yard-high cedar tree near by. He bounced off of it and scampered away without pause of any kind. It was as if he had "hit the ground running."

Few of us Christians meet persecution with the keep-running spirit. Our desire is to lie where we've fallen and nurse our injuries. We want someone to come with a stretcher and bear us carefully away. To accept adversity, not with negative self-pity or passive resentment, but with positive action, was Christ's way. He urged: "Love your enemies, bless them that curse you, do good to them that hate you" (Matt. 5:44). Paul exhorted: "If thine enemy hunger, feed him; if he thirst, give him drink: for in so doing thou shalt heap coals of fire on his head" (Rom. 12:20). Either one means that the Christian "hits the ground running."

To THINK ABOUT: *When circumstances give me a tumble, do I give up, or do I get up and keep going through faith in God?*

To PRAY ABOUT: *Lord, help me to press on regardless of bumps or bruises.*

ROTTEN SEED

WE'D OPENED a trench the length of the garden and had been dropping beans into it. But we ran out of beans before we reached the end of the long row. I went to hunt some beans left over from last year's planting. They didn't look very healthy, but we took a chance and finished out the row.

When, after a reasonable interval of time, no sprouts appeared at that end of the row, we dug up some of the seeds to see what they were doing. Instead of sprouting they were rotting.

The Bible would have termed that seed "corruptible" as over against the kind that is "incorruptible": "Being born again, not of corruptible seed but of incorruptible, by the word of God which liveth and abideth forever" (I Pet. 1:23).

Many people are not "born again" because the incorruptible seed of the gospel is neglected in favor of the corruptible seed of good works, respectable citizenship, church affiliation, rites and rituals, doing the best you can, or some other substitute. Only the shed blood of the Lord Jesus Christ, accepted in faith as the one atonement for sin, is effective in begetting spiritual life: "Ye were not redeemed with corruptible things, as silver and gold, from your vain conversation received by tradition from your fathers; but with the precious blood of Christ, as of a lamb without blemish and without spot" (I Pet. 1:18–19).

To THINK ABOUT: *Have I been depending on corruptible seed to produce spiritual life?*

To PRAY ABOUT: *Lord, plant in my heart the incorruptible seed of the true gospel.*

LUSH PASTURES

THE SPRING rains green up the pastures until each one is a miniature Ireland. We turn the cattle onto the native grass and keep them shut out of the planted "permanent" pastures. These will be harvested to provide hay for next winter; their second growth, after the cutting, will provide fall forage. Thus the cattle go in and out from one fenced field to another, and each time find lush, green pasture in abundance.

Christ says: "I am the door: by me if any man enter in, he shall be saved, and shall go in and out, and find pasture" (John 10:9).

I've always appreciated the progression outlined in that verse. First, through faith in Christ we are saved. A relationship is established. Born into the family of God through spiritual regeneration, we become His sons and heirs.

After that, and not before, we can find pasture. Our spiritual nature is nourished on His Word. In the Bible we find enlightenment, strength, and satisfaction such as has never before been ours. In the pasture of His choice we have fellowship with our Lord Jesus Christ. Then the Twenty-third Psalm becomes a personal experience. To go in and out at the Shepherd's bidding is not a matter of restraint but of liberty. The fences are not to keep us in, but to keep evil out. The fold is not a prison but a protection.

To THINK ABOUT: *Have I been resenting the Shepherd's care, mistaking it for coercion?*

To PRAY ABOUT: *Lord, help me to acquiesce in Your "pasture plan" for my life.*

MAY

THIS IS posy month. There are irises of varying colors. There are tulips; we favor the raggedy-edged parrot species. In bouquets they go well with bridal wreath or snowballs or mock orange. Hollyhocks have raised their spires along the retaining wall, and the Paul's scarlet and purple clematis are decking the porches and trellises with their bright blooms. Pink peonies, great oversize beauties as well as snowy white ones, come at the last, along with myriads of daisies.

But May is not all blossoms and soft breezes. It's the month for struggling with weeds and listening for possible tornado warnings. The beetles and blight have to be reckoned with, and the webworms and wild predators. The cattle get an obsession that grass is greener on the other side of the fence, and slyly escape our boundaries. That means fence lines have to be run, sometimes checked more than once before we find where they get out.

There's strong internal conflict too; the yearning to "play hooky" and go fishing, boating, picnicking, or hiking—versus the obligation to hoe, harrow, or hammer; clean, cook or churn.

Often we remain at our duties until sundown, then get in the boat and glide into the sunset. We may even linger on until the moon comes up to gild the waves and etch the landscape with silver while we drift and dream, letting Him communicate to our spirits the meaning of the day.

WE MAY GET IN THE BOAT AND
GLIDE INTO THE SUNSET

TREE FROGS

This time of year the "singing" of the tree frogs nearly splits our eardrums. But if they didn't sing, we would probably never know they exist, so cleverly do they conceal themselves. Their color merges with that of their surroundings, a bit of vegetation or a tree trunk, making them most difficult to spy. To aid them in their tree climbing, they have adhesive discs on their toes and fingers. In contrast to some other frog species, they lay very few eggs. But instead of laying them where fish and insects would be apt to devour a large portion of them, the tree frog builds a special nursery. Using mud, she constructs a low-walled enclosure at the water's edge in shallow water, and deposits the eggs within it, attaching them to grass or leaves. There the tadpoles can emerge in comparative safety and remain until they are capable of caring for themselves in deeper water.

God meant for human parents to provide for the welfare of their children too during the formative years. He has established an effective method for putting a protective wall around them: "These words, which I command thee this day, shall be in thine heart: And thou shalt teach them diligently unto thy children, and shalt talk of them when thou sittest in thine house, and when thou walkest by the way, and when thou liest down, and when thou risest up" (Deut. 6:6–7). Children tutored in that manner will escape many dangers and temptations which might otherwise destroy them.

To think about: *If it is criminal negligence to deprive a child physically of light, food, clothing, and exercise, what must it be to deprive him spiritually?*

To pray about: *Lord, help me to use Your Word to safeguard children.*

GOD'S PLOWBOYS

I WENT out early on a damp morning to pick up night crawlers for fish bait. These huge earthworms come to the surface after a rain, but can burrow back into the earth surprisingly fast when you try to catch them.

If you look closely, here and there around the yard you can see tiny mounds of fine particles of earth which have been piled up as a result of their activity. "God's plowboys" someone has called them, and not without reason, for their action has much to do with the breakdown of organic matter and the fertility of the soil. It has been estimated that with fifty thousand worms to an acre, eighteen tons of earth casting result in a year—enough to deposit a new, rich, three-inch layer of topsoil in a twenty-year period. On that basis, a worm has more influence on a country's economy than a lion or an elephant. A force need not be large in bulk to have power and effect.

"Who hath despised the day of small things?" (Zech. 4:10). God has declared that it is apt to be the little and humble people rather than the great and mighty who will be useful to Him. "Base things of the world, and things which are despised, hath God chosen . . . to bring to nought things that are" (I Cor. 1:28). Nothing is too little or insignificant for His use.

To THINK ABOUT: *Have I been using my littleness or weakness for an alibi?*

To PRAY ABOUT: *Use me, Lord, though small and insignificant, for Your purposes.*

WHITECAPS

When the wind whips up a storm on the lake we sometimes watch boaters hurrying for shelter. One time a fisherman's motor stopped, and I could see him laboring at the oars. All around him the waves were tossing and frothing. "Whitecaps" we call them, when they get like that. Though the man's identity was unknown to me, I prayed for his safety and wished I could be of other help. I could imagine what it was like, pulling desperately on the oars, yet making no progress, hearing the hissing of the water as waves broke over the prow of the boat.

There were once some frightened fishermen, storm-tossed on the Sea of Galilee. "In the fourth watch of the night Jesus went unto them, walking on the sea . . . saying, Be of good cheer; it is I; be not afraid." Then Peter, upon Jesus' encouragement, started to walk to Him on the water. "But when he saw the wind boisterous, he was afraid" (Matt. 14:25–31).

For a time faith had been Peter's life jacket, giving him buoyancy. But, taking his eyes off of Jesus, his faith was punctured. His doubts were sinking him. Before it was completedly deflated, however, such faith as was left cried out to Jesus to save him. His little faith was honored.

To think about: *What doubts (about God's mercy, power, love, wisdom, guidance, providence) are sinking me today?*

To pray about: *Lord, help me to keep my eyes upon You in full faith.*

OAK APPLES

MONG spring's oddities are the fuzzy, spherical, pink and white pompons about two inches in diameter which appear on oak trees. They are so attractive, and their colors so delicate, that I sometimes include them in floral arrangements.

Actually, they are galls made by the larvae of the woolsower insect. While the oak stem was young and tender it was "stung" by the adult insect in the process of depositing its eggs. When the eggs hatch into larvae they extrude matter which makes the pompon. So if you break a pompon open you will find it alive with crawlers inside.

The world is concerned mostly with the outward aspects of life, the part that is manifest. But the Bible evaluates people according to what is inside them and hidden. "Their inward part is very wickedness" (Ps. 5:9). Christ denounced false prophets in these terms: "Inwardly they are ravening wolves" (Matt. 7:15).

Public acts are really the outgrowth of private beliefs. To alter acts we must transform thoughts and emotions. This can only come about as human hearts are regenerated by the Holy Spirit, through faith in Christ Jesus.

To THINK ABOUT: *Am I more concerned about what man sees on the outside than about what God sees in my heart?*

To PRAY ABOUT: *Create in me a clean heart, O God, and renew a right spirit within me.*

SNAIL'S PACE

WANDERING in the woods I came upon the pretty little whorled abode of a land snail. It was thin, like eggshell china, delicately veined and gracefully spiraled. Snails can't live where there isn't enough limestone for their do-it-yourself style of home building. It seems strange that a creature which can produce something as durable and artistic as this shell should be looked down on because it is slow-moving. We'd be slow too, if we had to lay our own pavement as we traveled.

Anyway, is a faster pace as desirable as we're often led to imagine? Why is such a premium placed on speed? In order to speed up our lives we are condensing books, foods, procedures, all sorts of things. In so doing we are sacrificing much that is worth while—fellowship with our children who all too soon will be grown up and gone, enjoyment of the wonderful world around us, even communion with God and meditation on His Word.

"The race is not to the swift" (Eccles. 9:11). And because of that very fact Paul exhorts: "Walk in wisdom toward them that are without, redeeming the time" (Col. 4:5). If we are to redeem the time for the things of eternity, we shall have to slow down and omit some of the things of the present world.

To THINK ABOUT: *What important things of the Spirit have I omitted in order to "save" time to squander for Satan?*

To PRAY ABOUT: *Lord, help me to slow down and live a life worth while to You.*

69

SOMETHING AS DURABLE
YET ARTISTIC AS THE SNAIL'S SHELL

CROW SENTINELS

THE CROWS are with us the year round, droll and audacious, ruthless and clever. Many's the tale of their mischief and trickery. Everyone agrees they're hard to outwit. Scarecrows have little, if any, effect on them.

Though there's much to their discredit, they are reputed to be good "family men," willing to help incubate the eggs and raise the young. And they seem to have strong ties of loyalty to one another.

They travel in groups, and whenever there is a project afoot, two or three of their number are left as sentries. They are very alert. At the slightest token of danger they sound an alarm to warn the rest of the flock.

God's children are not quite so dependable in the matter of warning their fellows, yet the Scripture considers it vital: "When I say unto the wicked, thou shalt surely die; and thou givest him not warning, nor speakest to warn the wicked from his wicked way, to save his life; the same wicked man shall die in his iniquity; but his blood will I require at thine hand" (Ezek. 3:18). The apostle Paul cleared himself in that respect, and he did so in a spirit of love: "Therefore watch, and remember that by the space of three years I ceased not to warn every one night and day with tears" (Acts 20:31). God's people today should have as great a concern, lest all about us men die in their wickedness, unwarned.

To THINK ABOUT: *Whose blood is upon my hands, because I have not spoken up?*

To PRAY ABOUT: *Lord, lay upon my heart the identity of those persons whom it is my responsibility to warn, and enable me to do it with tenderness, love, and tears.*

NEGLECTING TO WEED

I WATCHED a neighbor's method of gardening. To prepare his seedbeds he plowed, broke up clods, and removed stones. He read directions and followed the horticultural suggestions which applied to what he was planting. When his plants appeared, he saw to it that they had the required moisture; he irrigated if necessary. He did everything that was proper and right.

But when the weeds appeared, he neglected them, even when they were so small they could have been picked with a minimum of effort. Later they were too strongly rooted to pull. Attacking them with a hoe frequently did more damage than good. At length he lost most of his crops to the weeds, which choked out and overran his garden.

Many couples practice parenthood in the same manner. They make great preparations for the coming of their child. After its arrival there is diligent care in regard to diet, pleasant surroundings, and cultural advantages. But what of the weeds which would choke its development, and ultimately ruin its future? What about trashy literature, pointless if not actually injurious television programs, questionable pastimes?

So much has been said in this modern era about emphasizing the positive, that it has become customary to ignore the negative. However, that is a violation of Scripture: "Bring them up in the nurture and admonition of the Lord" (Eph. 6:4). The root meaning of admonish is gently or mildly to rebuke or reprove, to warn against. There must plainly be negative admonition as well as positive nurture.

TO THINK ABOUT: *Are we permitting the weeds to take the garden of a child's life?*

TO PRAY ABOUT: *Lord, help us to maintain a proper balance of both positive and negative emphasis in our children's upbringing.*

SKIN DIVERS

SKIN DIVING is popular in our area. With "lungs" (tanks of oxygen) fastened to their backs as a means of breathing swimmers descend to great depths.

But men aren't as original as they like to think. The whirligig beetle has been skin diving since long before man ever thought of trying it. These shiny black insects can be seen skimming the surface of many a pond or pool. They don't need to carry any special container for their oxygen. They just keep a bubble of air tucked under their wing cases at all times. When danger threatens they promptly dive and draw on the bubble for air to breathe while they are submerged.

God has given the Christian a means of "breathing" despite the pressure of trouble. He ordained prayer, "the breath of the soul," as the Christian's constant air supply: "Call upon me in the day of trouble: I will deliver thee, and thou shalt glorify me" (Ps. 50:15). "It shall come to pass, that before they call I will answer: and while they are yet speaking, I will hear" (Isa. 65:24). God is there with help and succor. His resources for new life are at hand. Our part is to appropriate them.

TO THINK ABOUT: *Is God really with me at all times, even when things seem to get me down?*

TO PRAY ABOUT: *Lord, teach me to pray, and there to find new strength for my soul.*

SALTING THE COWS

ONE OF OUR periodic chores is that of placing a block of salt in the pasture where the cattle can lick it to obtain needed minerals. We suspect the deer of using it too, and maybe other animals, for all we know. It would be interesting to know how many are actually served by it.

Jesus said to those who believed in Him: "Ye are the salt of the earth" (Matt. 5:13). I think the Bible contains no simpler or clearer passage setting forth what the Christian is supposed to be and do.

Salt is valuable for many purposes. It preserves from corruption; that is why ham is cured, fish and pickles brined, and so on. Salt checks infection; that is why the doctor orders people with sore throats to gargle with salt water. Salt melts ice, so we put it on icy doorsteps or driveways. Salt imparts flavor; many food substances would be unpalatable without it. Salt creates a thirst, making the user crave water.

But as Jesus continues in the same passage: "If the salt have lost his savour, wherewith shall it be salted? It is thenceforth good for nothing, but to be cast out, and to be trodden under foot of men" (Matt. 5:13).

To THINK ABOUT: *In what ways am I functioning as God's salt in my community?*

To PRAY ABOUT: *Lord, help me really to be "salt of the earth," fit for something besides being cast underfoot.*

JUNE

THIS IS FRUIT month. Most of both the wild and the cultivated ones mature now. All afford treats for the eye as well as for the palate. The blackberry bushes bend gracefully with the weight of bright red, half-ripe berries intermingled with the glossy black of the ripe ones. Gooseberries are perfect little globes of green until they swell and ripen to a dark, dull red. The currants come in two varieties, small and red, and large and black.

The birds nearly always beat us to the cherries. We do well if we have a few to eat off the tree. Plums come yellow, green, red, and deep purple. Black raspberries have a frosty look on both stems and berries. Served with thick cream, they are top eating.

Huckleberries are so tedious to pick we don't spare time to gather many from the rocky ridges. I do enjoy bringing home branches of them for floral arrangements. One stem will bear fruit in all stages of development: green, yellow, pink, purple, black. But the color names do not do justice to their beauty. Early peaches follow next, juicy golden spheres blushed pink on one cheek.

All these fruits make beautiful jewel-toned jellies, syrupy jams, rich preserves, and canned or frozen stores from which to conjure pies and cobblers.

It all sounds wonderful, but every bit of beauty and every bite of bounty demands a corresponding cost in briar-scratched arms, punctured fingers, chigger-bitten bodies, long hours in the kitchen at sink and stove, numerous trips up and down basement stairs, and end-of-the-day fatigue when you can only tumble groaning into bed.

Yet you thank God for His generosity, and whether you're working indoors or out-doors, there are meditations inspired by your experiences.

FRESH DAILY

WHEN A FRIEND arrived for a visit the other day, she handed us a pink pasture rose and a stalk of blue spiderwort which she had picked along the road as she came. The color combination was pleasing, and I put them in a vase in the kitchen window. Before she left, our visitor remarked that the spiderwort flowerets looked as if they were already fading, while the wild rose was as fresh as ever.

The next morning, however, I observed that the rose petals had fallen to the window sill, leaving only the unlovely center, so I plucked the stem from the vase and cast it into the trash basket. The spiderwort stalk, on the other hand, displayed a new blossom, bright in its fresh-opened blueness. The next morning there was another to take its place, and it in turn was replaced by a fourth new bloom on the morning after that.

"It is of the Lord's mercies that we are not consumed, because his compassions fail not. They are new every morning" (Lam. 3:22-23). As each day dawns, more sure than the daily delivery of newspaper, mail, or milk, there is God's mercy, fitted to the day's need for each one of us individually. "Great is thy faithfulness." And every child of God is a recipient of it.

To THINK ABOUT: *Do I "collect" God's daily mercy as promptly as I do the daily paper or milk?*

To PRAY ABOUT: *Lord, help me to appreciate the timeliness and constancy of Your blessings.*

DEW-SPANGLED WEB

WE WENT OUT this morning and found everything bejeweled with dew. On the crosspieces of porch and boat dock, between electric lines, and suspended from branches of trees—in fact all around us—were beautifully symmetrical triangular, quadrangular, or polygonal spider webs. The radiating foundation lines in webs are inelastic and non-adhesive. But the spiral lines going in the other direction, so fascinatingly equidistant, are sticky, which means woe to the insect that blunders into them.

Vibrations set up by the struggling prey signal the hidden spider of his catch. By a single thread, which is his trap line, and which provides a passage for the spider from his hide-out, he hastens out to devour his captive.

Satan is just as clever. His snares are as attractive and at the same time as entangling as the symmetry and stickiness of the spider's web. He too lurks near by, ready to possess those who have been "taken captive by him at his will" (II Tim. 2:26). He too will destroy his prey. "Be sober, be vigilant: because your adversary the devil, as a roaring lion, walketh about, seeking whom he may devour" (I Pet. 5:8). And his snare may be just as deceptively destructive as the dew-spangled web.

TO THINK ABOUT: *Are the difficulties in which I become trapped the result of my own willfulness or disobedience?*

PRAYER: *Lord, help me to be alert to escape entanglement in Satan's snares.*

THE STICKY SPIRAL LINES MEAN WOE TO
THE INSECTS THAT BLUNDER INTO THEM

MIRRORED SKY

THE LAKE's reflection of the sky is one of our beauties. It gives us so many double-takes of loveliness. On a clear, still night we can see the individual stars mirrored in the water's placid surface. They make it look like a sequined drape. Sometimes the early morning sky, wearing pink and pastel tints like the inside of a shell, is reflected again in the lake. Only on the blue water the bright pink becomes a delicate amethyst; otherwise the image below is identical with the original above.

Christ is just such a reflection of God: "The brightness of his glory, and the express image of his person" (Heb. 1:3). And just as we have seen the sky, so to speak, when we have seen its reflection in the lake, so, said Christ, "He that hath seen me hath seen the Father" (John 14:9). Thus it is, that whatever we would like to know about God, we can discover in Christ. Do you want to know how merciful God is? Think of Christ's compassion and you have the measure. Do you want to know how mighty God is? Think of Christ's miraculous power and you have the answer.

TO THINK ABOUT: *Have I missed knowing all I might about God because I haven't been familiar enough with Christ?*

TO PRAY ABOUT: *Lord, help me to lay hold of Your reality through Christ.*

TRUMPET VINES

THE ORANGE trumpet flowers are a common summer sight along road and lake shore in our area. We have a couple of vines near the house which climb its walls and shade bedroom and kitchen windows. I don't know whether they were planted there or volunteered.

Every so often at junctures between vine and branches, they put out fine root-like growths which have great clinging power. By these they will attach themselves to the siding of the house or the window screen, and it is only with difficulty that their grip is broken. I have often marvelled at the ability of such small grippers to support such a heavy growth of vine and hold it fast to the house.

Christians exercise the same sort of hold. "Let us hold fast the profession of our faith without wavering" (Heb. 10:23). "Hold fast the form of sound words, which thou hast heard of me, in faith and love which is in Christ Jesus" (II Tim. 1:13). Our profession of faith, if it is genuine, is based on the sound words of the gospel transmitted to us through faithful preachers.

TO THINK ABOUT: *Is my grip on the gospel strong enough to support me in Christian growth?*

TO PRAY ABOUT: *Lord, help me in word and act to hold fast my Christian profession and not to waver.*

VULTURE'S FEET

TURKEY VULTURES, or buzzards, as they are also called, are carrion-feeding birds remarkable for their telescopic eyesight and their graceful flight. The tales of their amazing vision are endless. One has only to watch them briefly to be convinced of their aerial prowess. They wheel so dexterously, glide so effortlessly, and then swoop so accurately upon their prey.

Nevertheless, they have their deficiency, and it's in their feet. An owl can drive its claws through a man's wrist as if it were tissue paper. A hawk can carry prey almost as large as itself. An eagle can wield its talons so ferociously that most animals fear to attack it. But the buzzard's feet are weak as tools and powerless as weapons.

In a spiritual sense the Christian is weak and powerless in his feet too, except as he depends on God to make his feet function as they should. "The Lord God is my strength, and he will make my feet like hinds' feet, and he will make me to walk upon mine high places" (Hab. 3:19). "Thou hast enlarged my steps under me that my feet did not slip" (Ps. 18:36). It is God who must empower our feet to progress in the path of His will rather than slide backward into temptation.

TO THINK ABOUT: *Are my feet weak when it comes to taking me places I should go for Jesus' sake?*

TO PRAY ABOUT: *Lord, strengthen me to walk today in the path You have set for me.*

WATERLOGGED BOATS

IVING ON the lake as we do, we find that boats are an important piece of equipment. They must be taken care of and kept in good condition. This means that after heavy rainstorms they have to be bailed and sponged out. Sometimes I lend a hand with the task.

"A boat's no good except in the water, but it's worse than no good if the water's in it." I once heard that familiar saying applied to a Christian. If the believer withdraws from society and secludes himself as a hermit, or even as an ascetic in a cloister with others, his life is not available to God for witnessing to Christ-less men.

On the other hand, if the Christian has the world in himself, he impairs his testimony, for the unbeliever can see no difference in their respective lives. The boat must be in the water, but not have the water in it. "Love not the world, neither the things that are in the world. If any man love the world, the love of the Father is not in him" (I John 2:15). "Be not conformed to this world: but be ye transformed by the renewing of your mind, that ye may prove what is that good, and acceptable, and perfect, will of God" (Rom. 12:2). If the things of the world are predominant in me, then I am not in the perfect will of God.

TO THINK ABOUT: *Am I, because of worldliness, unfit for God's use, like a boat that is waterlogged?*

TO PRAY ABOUT: *Lord, show me the places where the world is seeping into my life, and by Your Holy Spirit enable me to stop the seepage.*

HAWK MOTH

THE MIMOSA tree is in full dress. Every branch tip is a fluff of rosy bloom beckoning hummingbird and bumblebee to come tipple nectar at its bar. One customer is the huge hawk or sphinx moth which vibrates his dark, tapered wings so fast that he is easily mistaken for a hummingbird.

His life history is an interesting one. The eggs are laid and hatched out on tomato vines (and some other plants such as tobacco). There the bright green caterpillar which emerges from them soon gorges himself to considerable size on the leaves. Then, burrowing six or seven inches into the ground, the worm pupates in a dark, reddish-brown chrysalis from which it eventually emerges a fat-bodied moth, with a wingspread of around four inches.

The most remarkable thing in the moth's anatomy is the tubular mouth it has rolled up under its head like a watch spring. This proboscis is a sucking apparatus for extracting nectar from deep-throated flowers like the morning-glory, petunia, trumpet, honeysuckle, and some varieties of orchids. It is by this means that many flowers are fertilized. Some species cannot be pollinated by any other natural means.

Here is another evidence that God provides a resource for every need. Why can't we humans believe that fact and apply it with assurance in our lives? Is it not written: "My God shall supply all your need according to his riches in glory by Christ Jesus" (Phil. 4:19)?

TO THINK ABOUT: *Am I worrying about things instead of counting on the God who made provision for the orchid's pollination?*

TO PRAY ABOUT: *God, supply my need according to Your riches.*

PET COMPANIONS

SOMETIMES the lake water becomes muddied by heavy and continued rains. Then the fishing is good only where fresh water comes in. At such times the place where the creek water empties into our arm of the lake becomes a rendezvous for numerous boatloads of fishers angling for white bass. The occasion becomes quite social in nature because everyone visits with everyone else, compares catches, relates fish stories, and prognosticates what tomorrow's weather or fishing prospects will be.

We have found that people most often determine our identity, not by the color or size of our boat, or our own physical features, but by the presence of our dog Tigie. She loves to go boating, and regardless of weather or temperature, she insists on accompanying us. The minute the boat heads away from the dock, she drapes herself across the prow until we reach a fishing spot. After we have anchored, she may seek shade under one of the seats, but often she remains at the bow the whole time.

Christians often have pets that identify them, pet habits, that is. "She's the woman who's always making catty remarks." "He's the man who has such a trigger temper and is always losing it." The beloved disciple John had a habit of leaning on Jesus' breast. Martha's sister Mary had a habit of taking her place at His feet. People can be identified by such habits.

Mutual love is the habit that is supposed to identify Christians. "By this shall all men know that ye are my disciples, if ye have love one to another" (John 13:35).

To THINK ABOUT: *Do my habits identify me with the world or with Christ?*

To PRAY ABOUT: *Lord, let Your love be made manifest in me as an indication to all men, and to me, that I am Yours.*

TURTLE TALE

I WAS AT the kitchen sink the other morning when I heard my father loudly calling my name from down on the dock. I dashed out the door, and as I ran, could see he was struggling with something, for his fish pole was bent double by whatever he was trying to land. I grabbed the net and helped him get his catch ashore. It was a turtle weighing around fifteen pounds. We all discussed what to do with it. I was for dressing it, so the men cut off its head.

As it was the time of morning when the white bass strike best, we decided to let the turtle lie while we went fishing. Upon our return we set about to dress it. It had been three or four hours since the "critter's" head had been cut off, but his reflexes were still in operation. When we took hold of him to start to cut, the turtle's big claws opened. We involuntarily jerked back in fright and dropped him. When we tried it again, the same thing happened. It was a laughable sight, but it became serious as an illustration of myself and of the sin that will not die within me.

At Calvary my old nature has been slain: "Our old man is crucified with him, that the body of sin might be destroyed, that henceforth we should not serve sin. For he that is dead is freed from sin" (Rom. 6:6). Nevertheless, the "motions of sin" are still manifest in me because, like Paul, "what I would, that I do not; but what I hate, that do I" (Rom. 7:15). But, praise God, just as a headless turtle can do no real harm, so because of the cross where the serpent's head was bruised, "sin shall not have dominion over me" (Rom. 6:14).

To THINK ABOUT: *What motions of the old man of sin are still manifest in me?*

To PRAY ABOUT: *Lord, I thank You for the victory won through Christ.*

MOSQUITO LAUNCH

IN THE summertime here on the lake we would be devoured by mosquitoes were it not for the spray control program. Every week to ten days a motorboat equipped with heavy hose tipped with a large nozzle makes the rounds. As it approaches our cove, machinery is put into operation which shoots a fuel oil mixture through the hose. The stream of insecticide is played clear up to the head of the cove, spraying thoroughly the entire shoreline and water surface. This practice effectively destroys all the mosquito larvae which may be developing in the shallow waters. If the young are killed, there can be no adult insects to annoy us or spread disease.

Totalitarian governments employ similar tactics. By direct and devious methods they seek to keep young people away from church. They assume that by killing off the young in faith they will eventually stamp out Christianity. The success of their scheme will be in direct proportion to the faithfulness or negligence of the parents in giving spiritual instruction in the home.

God said, "Train up a child in the way he should go: and when he is old he will not depart from it" (Prov. 22:6). He said to parents: "Tell ye your children of it, and let your children tell their children, and their children another generation" (Joel 1:3). In these admonitions God was anticipating just such a situation as exists in totalitarian countries today, but not only there! And He was ordaining a counteroperation.

To THINK ABOUT: *Are we leaving the spiritual training of our children entirely to agencies outside the home?*

To PRAY ABOUT: *Lord, help us to fulfil our obligation to nurture the spiritual lives of our children.*

SUMMER

SUMMER

G OD'S WORLD is not only crowded with beauty to behold, it also vibrates with fascinating sounds to be heard. There's the mysterious realm of the super- or ultrasonic of both nature and civilization that scientists are just beginning to investigate by means of intricate recording mechanisms. To us common folks, however, God has given a marvelous organ called the ear which is capable of receiving an intriguing range of tones.

Listen with me to a portion of what just one summer day has to offer:

Predawn: I stir drowsily. A cool breeze blows through the open window and across my body. Liquid melody pours forth gloriously from the throat of a mockingbird in the multiflora rose thicket, himself as gray as the advancing dawn. I drowse, floating in a cascading river of trills and cadences.

5 a.m.: I stir again, open one eye clockward, close it again, and pretend it is not yet time to get up. I hear the guttural cry of a great blue heron stalking along the shallow edge of the cove, searching the water for his breakfast. A short shriek means a kingfisher is cursing over his faulty swoop for a fish.

6 a.m.: The bird symphony is in full chorus as I put the coffee water on to heat. The cardinals in the woods flute cheerily, a blackbird does a reed obligato, and a phoebe on the electric line contributes his monotonous two-tone accompaniment, while the sparrows under the eaves fiddle tweet-tweet, and a woodpecker in the hollow tree drums out the rhythm.

7 a.m.: I toss some laundry into the washer and run water over the breakfast dishes. From just across the cove, in through the open window, comes the clear call of the quail: "Bobwhite! Bobwhite!" He's probably a widower in the briar patch courting a second mate, though that seems an unlikely place for romance.

8 a.m.: I step out with the garbage and hear the staccato bark of a fox squirrel. His sleek red coat gleams in the morning sun as he sits on an oak limb conversing in code with the bright-eyed coquette in the walnut tree. In a near-by elm, a titmouse yodels with all the surprising volume of his two tiny lungs.

9 a.m.: I sally forth to hang up some clothes. On a near-by pole a saucy wren teeters to give me a repetitious dissertation on "Teakettle! Teakettle! Teakettle!" Across the cove some crows, shamelessly bathing in public, hurl ribald quips at one another.

10 a.m.: While I am out on the porch to shake a throw rug, there is a whir-r-r of wee wings as a hummingbird helicopters over the honeysuckle vine. Fanning up a much noisier swish of air, the flock of guineas thunder in from foraging afar. From over in the pasture comes a faint, worried "Moo?" Bossy has mislaid her new calf and is inquiring as to its whereabouts.

11 a.m.: Plying the dust mop on the sun porch where all the windows are open to the outdoor opera, I hear the sun-sparkled waves lap the shore with the smack of hungry lips.

12 noon: Time enough to sweep the back steps while the potatoes boil. "Meow! Meow!" Pussy cat reproaches me for not having provided an early lunch. As I wield the broom I hear a pulsing roar and look up to see white tracks laid across the sky's blue roadbed by a jet's twin vapor trails.

1 p.m.: We linger over the lunch table, lulled to inactivity by the monotonous hum of insects. Now and then, from under some stone in the walk, comes the cheery chirp of a cricket, lending accent to the droning of bumblebees in the mimosa blooms.

2 p.m.: As I unpin white billows from the clothesline, I hear a silken rustle on the ground and look down to see a garter snake slithering by. While I pause to admire his bright green and yellow skin I hear the leaves overhead whispering secrets to each other.

3 p.m.: Walking down an old road I am brought to a halt by the angry cheep-cheep of a chipmunk who challenges my right to trespass on his personal precincts.

4 p. m.: I continue cautiously, not wanting to arouse the ire of any other of the rural residents. Then I pause, detecting a slight, agitated trot-trot, punctuated by low notes of distress. Yonder is a wild turkey, momentarily panicked by a woven wire fence. A concerned tom turkey over the ridge, making intermittent gobble-gobbles, invites her to soar to him.

5 p.m.: Leisurely, with only the soft scuff of my feet on the grass violating the silence, I wander homeward beneath the forest trees. In their boughs, hidden musicians now and then tune their instruments. Off in the pasture, a field sparrow practices its scales, always beginning at the top and descending in harmony.

6 p.m.: As the foamy yellow milk I am straining gurgles into earthen crocks, a distant motorboat sets reverberations rolling across the lake.

7 p.m.: A tree frog unbuttons his accordion and splits the air with its echoes while I shut up shop for the night in the kitchen.

8 p.m.: Wearily I drop into an easy chair on the sun porch prepared to relax and read. Outside the cicadas set up their strident hum like the chant of a lynching mob frenziedly demanding, "We want so and so. We want so and so."

9 p.m.: A mosquito, sole survivor of the spray control program, sings his satisfaction in my ear. I reach up and turn off the light. Maybe that will assure *my* escape. He seems to have been detoured. For some unknown reason there is a brief respite from the scream of the cicadas too. I settle back and relax. I close my eyes to enjoy the silence. Abruptly it is ruptured. A paddlefish has leaped from the water, pivoted,

90

and plunged back into the depths with an accompanying slap of spanked water. A bullfrog on the shore hoarsely applauds the performance.

10 p.m.: From afar comes a wretched request: "Whippoorwill! Whippoorwill!" Closer by comes a companion query that sends chills chasing down the spine. "Who-oo-oo? Who-oo-oo?" asks a little screech owl.

"Not I," is my dreamy retort as I drift into peaceful slumber.

JULY

THE MIDSUMMER months are times of conservation. Poultry has to be readied for the deep freeze, also vegetables. There's kraut to make, tomatoes to can, berries to jell and preserve, cucumbers and beets to pickle. Heat, sometimes drouth, and always chiggers, complicate living. The war with weeds must still be waged and greens must be mowed.

Then comes haying and its accompanying hubbub and fatigue. That seems unavoidable even if crews come in and do the job for you. There's still spraying for borers and dusting for beetles to be done, while the tomato vines must be watched and the voracious hornworms hand-picked from them.

But there are butterflies as well as caterpillars: the lovely lemon yellow swallowtails, once in a while a gorgeous green luna moth brought in from the woods. The phlox, dahlias, balsam, gladioli, rose of Sharon, regal and day lilies provide pollen for the winged creatures. The naked lady, surprise, or resurrection lily (whichever is your name for the hardy amaryllis) suddenly adds its pale pink petals to the scene.

Squirrel and frog season open. If there's time for it, trotlines may be strung in hopes of landing a giant flathead catfish. We may get a bizarre paddlefish instead, or be fortunate enough to get a channel or blue catfish as a more prized trophy. Or if there is opportunity to be that indolent, we simply bait a heavy line, tie it to an empty glass jug, and toss the whole of it out of the boat, then lean back and doze until the jug begins to move away, whereupon we pull in our fish—maybe.

Mostly there's no time for such foolery. We keep on the bob all day, drop exhausted into bed at night, and fall asleep thanking Him for His management of the day's affairs and for their import in our lives.

PRUNING TIME

IN BLOSSOM time our mock orange is a delight to behold. Some of the branches are man high, so that it completely screens the thousand-gallon propane gas tank which holds our fuel. When the shrubs become loaded with blooms, it is a bower of beauty. Looking out the window at it sometimes seems like staring into a blizzard.

When the blooming season is over, however, must come the pruning. I get out the big snippers and commence cutting a branch here and a stalk there in order to remove the old wood. It is on the new growth that the blossoms come, and there will be no new growth except there be a cutting away of the old.

It always takes nerve to carry out this chore. I have a sort of heart failure, feeling as if I'm ruining the shrubs and that we'll never have posies again. But only once did we fail to have flowers; that was when I failed to prune.

God's pruning of the believer is vitally necessary. ". . . Every branch that beareth fruit, he purgeth it, that it may bring forth more fruit" (John 15:2).

TO THINK ABOUT: *Have I been guilty of rebellion against God's all-wise pruning for my Christian growth?*

TO PRAY ABOUT: *Lord, regardless of my reaction, continue the pruning process in order that I may be a more fruitful Christian.*

THE DARKER THE NIGHT,
THE WHITER LOOMS THE WAISTCOAT
OF THE BULLFROG

FROGS' LEGS

*O*CCASIONALLY friends come out from town to go frogging with us. There'll be two couples of us to sally forth in the boat. We take wraps because it's apt to turn chilly on the water, come midnight. One man sits at the stern and runs the motor. The other man straddles the bow. We women sit in the middle, help spot frogs, and manage to visit and giggle a good bit while doing it. Fortunately, silence is not an absolute requisite to success.

A dark night is. The darker the night, the whiter looms the waistcoat of the bullfrog on the bank. When one is spotted, the boat is eased toward him and the "frogger" at the prow snaps on a powerful flashlight, focusing its beams directly into the frog's eyes. Blinded by the rays, he is not aware that a hand had slipped around behind him until it closes tightly over his middle. He is still gasping hoarsely with astonishment when he is thrust into a gunny sack.

People can be blinded too. "If our gospel be hid, it is hid to them that are lost: In whom the god of this world hath blinded the minds of them which believe not" (II Cor. 4:3-4). "And no marvel; for Satan himself is transformed into an angel of light" (II Cor. 11:14).

Our pity is always kindled at the misfortune and handicap of a physically blind person. Far greater should be our concern for the spiritually blind all around us who have never known Christ.

To THINK ABOUT: *Are the "bright lights" of the world blinding me or my friends to Christ and what He has to offer?*

To PRAY ABOUT: *Lord, guard me from being entranced by any light but Your own.*

BRINGING BOATS TO DOCK

A SUDDEN severe storm came up the other day. Huge masses of clouds were dashing across the sky like chariots pulled by invisible horses. The wind began to blow and the waves rocked the dock until it creaked and groaned. Then the rain began to fall, making its own peculiar rustle as it came down in sheets.

We heard the snorting bark of a motor, and saw a boatful of people racing down the center of the lake arm. Apparently they realized that they could not outdistance the storm and make their home haven in time, for they soon swerved and headed for the shelter of our dock.

I went to greet them as they pulled into a stall of the dock, and was reminded of the time Jesus came walking on the waters to bring relief to the frightened disciples. "They willingly received him into the ship, and immediately the ship was at the land whither they went" (John 6:21).

We have no knowledge of the distance involved or the duration of the tempest on this occasion. But the Master's presence imparted progress and a safe docking at the desired destination. Always, if we will permit Him to come in as captain of our vessel, He will do the same for us.

To THINK ABOUT: *Am I laboring at the oars in my own strength, instead of receiving Jesus into the ship?*

To PRAY ABOUT: *Lord, help me to welcome, not fear, Your captaincy of my life.*

BINDWEED

GOT up early this morning and found there was a refreshing breeze which encouraged the young trees to try toe-bends. Little wavelets were rushing across the lake as if they were late for an appointment and trying to make up for lost time. The sun had not yet opened his eye, and a few clouds had their heads together as if conspiring to blindfold him when he did.

In view of the pleasant coolness, it seemed to be a good time to do some weeding in the garden. I pulled bindweed from the rain-softened soil and piled it in a bushel basket to feed to the chickens. The clinging, twisting grip of bindweed means eventual strangulation for the vegetable stalks around which it so tightly twines. Moreover, it cannot be treated with toxic spray. Whatever would penetrate and destroy it, would also destroy its host. The only way to deal with this strangling plant is to reach for the root and extract it.

Self-pity is the bindweed of the soul. It entwines the personality tighter and tighter until there can be no growth or expansion, merely self-involvement. Self-pity, however, will have no room to thrive in a soul garden that is plotted and set with thoughts of others. "Look not every man on his own things, but every man also on the things of others" (Phil. 2:4). "Let no man seek his own, but every man another's wealth" (I Cor. 10:24). The person who is busy carrying out these commands has no time to pity himself.

To think about: *How far up the stalk of my life have I permitted the bindweed of self-pity to twist itself?*

To pray about: *Lord, help me to be occupied with the welfare of others instead of self.*

FALLEN TREE

WE WERE down in one of the hollows near the brook checking the cattle when I noticed a large walnut tree lying prostrate on the bank. How it came to tumble we could not tell. What impressed me was that, though fallen, it was still green. Investigation revealed that one segment of root remained in the ground with its toes stretched toward the water. The tree could thus draw nourishment and moisture, even if it could not hold up its head to towering heights like the other forest trees.

Some of God's people are like that. They have been prostrated by ill health, bereavement, or other types of afflictions, but have kept sending up the green leaves of their testimony in spite of it. Strengthened by the power of prayer, and watered by the Word, they continue to grow and to fruit for Christ's sake.

They are like the "tree planted by the rivers of water, that bringeth forth his fruit in his season; his leaf also shall not wither, and whatsoever he doeth shall prosper" (Ps. 1:3). Our circumstances are never such but what we can bear fruit if we keep our roots in God.

To THINK ABOUT: *When circumstances prostrate me, do I still grow, or just groan?*

To PRAY ABOUT: *Lord, regardless of my situation, help me draw on You for power.*

DOUBLE VISION

WE KNEW it was the day for our milk cow to calve so we thought we had better look her up. In the way peculiar to such creatures, she had gone to the farthest reach of her pasture for the event. There we found it, a cute little calf, still damp, lying in the grass under the watchful surveillance of the proud mama. We especially noted its brown Jersey color because her previous calf had been black like its Angus sire.

Later, we decided we had better return with some dairy feed, so we made the long trek back to where we had first seen the calf. By now a light rain was falling. Did that account for what we saw? As we looked at the calf we were baffled to find it so much darker than it had seemed before. In fact, it was as black as its sire. How could that be?

We made a half turn to put the dairy feed before the cow, and rubbed our eyes. We were now looking at a Jersey-colored calf. Thus it was that we discovered there were twin calves: a heifer that looked like the mother, and a bull that resembled the father.

God had been asked for one good healthy calf and He had given two! He had doubled our blessings. He "is able to do exceeding abundantly above all that we ask or think" (Eph. 3:20). It is just like God to be that generous.

To THINK ABOUT: *Do I recognize all good fortune as a blessing come from the hand of God, and thank Him for it?*

To PRAY ABOUT: *Lord, create in me a thankful heart.*

AUGUST

HOSPITALITY is a year-round project with us, but sometimes in the summer months it becomes a slightly hectic activity. A Western Union boy doesn't ride up on a bicycle and hand us a telegram saying, "Arrive Thursday 2 p.m." Nor does the telephone ring and a voice inquire, "Will it be all right if we drive down tomorrow?" Instead, because of the unavailability of these two communication mediums in our area, our first intimation of guests may be when Tigie begins to bark. I look out the kitchen door and commence pulling at my clothes and struggling with my hair. I grab this and that, trying to tidy things up a bit, and glance at the clock to see how soon a meal will be in order.

We have learned to take frequent comings and goings somewhat in stride and be reconciled to it, because after all, the greatest satisfactions in life come from sharing. But occasionally we think it might have been helpful if sometime in our career we'd been hotel clerks during a simultaneous conclave of the Knights of the Protected Ark and a state basketball tournament, with a hardware dealer's convention thrown in for good measure.

One time it happened this way. We had just settled Aunt Clara and her brood in the guest cottage when the Vandeveres arrived to occupy the guest room. Then it proved to be the week end that a couple of boys attending the summer session at a near-by university elected to visit us. While I was mentally bedding them down on the sun porch I heard steps on the walk; some friends from town had guests of theirs "just out for a ride." While I was telling them about our guests, I caught a glimpse of their guests. My mouth dropped open as I recognized Tom and Polly from Peoria. For old times sake these friends too had to stay. I wouldn't have it any other way.

On such occasions it is with a good bit of maneuvering and not a little jolly hubbub that we get everyone arranged for and fed. After the evening meal's dishes have been washed and put away, we all gather on the sun porch. There may be no light except that of an insecticide candle (for it seems the little wingies will squeeze in despite screens). We exchange opinions on world affairs or just chit-chat about mutual friends or mutual interests.

Through the casement windows we can see the moon's spilled gold cascading across the lake and we can hear a gentle, lulling, lap-lap of the waves against the shore. The nighttime murmurs of the birds and bugs soothe the children into passivity. Presently they are asleep, and even the older heads begin to nod and drowse. Somehow the cares of life fall away like a wrap slipping from the shoulders.

The Book is brought and someone reads a chapter, reminding us anew of our wonderful Father and all He has done for us, and will yet do, because of His love and wisdom and power. We go to our respective beds relaxed and ready to sleep away the remaining hours of darkness with only our subconscious minds at work.

BARKING DOG

EVERY FARM, I guess, has its dog, and ours is no exception. A neighbor once asked me what ours was good for, and I could only answer, "To be loved," for we had never trained her for anything else, though she was smart enough to have learned.

She is obedient and loyal, and useful to a degree. No doubt her barking keeps many predators away from the chicken yard. Usually too, she barks to let us know of the arrival of visitors. If she ever fails to signal someone's arrival or approach, I feel as if she has played me false in permitting me to be come upon unawares.

In those rare instances she puts herself in a class with the dogs of Isaiah 56:10: "His watchmen are blind: they are all ignorant, they are all dumb dogs, they cannot bark; sleeping, lying down, loving to slumber."

It is to the discredit of the human race that this statement actually refers to people rather than dogs. And it is to the shame of Christians that we are so frequently dumb. We do not speak to warn the unbeliever of his need of Christ and of the fate that awaits men who do not receive Him.

TO THINK ABOUT: *Am I negligently at ease like a dumb dog instead of alertly witnessing for God?*

TO PRAY ABOUT: *Lord, help me to heed the Spirit's leadership and fulfil my responsibility as a watchman.*

INDIGO BUNTING

WHEN I CAN spare a few moments, I like to take the binoculars and go "birding." On one occasion, with my naked eye, I kept noticing a very dark bird flitting from tree to tree. I couldn't identify it and had difficulty getting a focus on it because it was doing so much moving about. When at last I got a good view of it through the glasses, I was very much surprised. It was not black at all, but blue, a very bright blue, and readily identifiable as an indigo bunting.

Many a circumstance in life looks black to us because we haven't the right focus or perspective on it. The old phrase, "a blessing in disguise," has scriptural validity.

Therefore it is well to talk to the Lord about the possible value of events before putting them down as troubles. It may be that our difficulties are permitted of God so that we can draw dividends on them. Our afflictions may in reality be assets. James counseled, "Consider it the purest joy, my brothers, when you are involved in various trials" (Jas. 1:2, Williams). "Our light affliction, which is but for a moment, worketh for us a far more exceeding and eternal weight of glory; while we look not at the things which are seen, but at the things which are not seen: for the things which are seen are temporal: but the things which are not seen are eternal" (II Cor. 4:17-18).

To THINK ABOUT: *Have I lacked the perspective of God's viewpoint to evaluate properly everyday occurrences?*

To PRAY ABOUT: *Lord, though I can't see through Your binoculars to distinguish between temporal "black" and eternal "blue," help me trust You anyway.*

ROCK MULCH

WE HAVE learned, particularly during the drouth years, how valuable a rock mulch can be. Flat rocks from six to twelve inches square are gathered from along the lake shore. They are laid around the base of a tree or shrub for a foot or two in all directions, fitted as closely together as their varying shapes permit.

This procedure helps in several ways. Most important, it preserves moisture. Not only that, but also growth of weeds which would choke the shrub or rob it of needed nutrients from the soil is retarded. Small animals are discouraged from molesting the plant. Altogether, rock mulching is a profitable practice.

While we were out in the boat the other evening, we stopped to select some rocks to use in this way. Just above the place where we were gathering the small rocks there towered the much larger rocks, some of them hollowed out by the water's action, others split in some unknown manner, but all of them capable of overshadowing and shielding a person.

According to Scripture, "My God is the rock of my refuge" (Ps. 94:22). "The Lord is my rock, and my fortress" (Ps. 18:2). "Lead me to the rock that is higher than I. For thou hast been a shelter for me, and a strong tower from the enemy" (Ps. 61:2-3). How blessed we are to have such a Rock for our protection!

TO THINK ABOUT: *Do I rebel at being overshadowed, or do I rejoice in the refuge of a strong tower?*

TO PRAY ABOUT: *Lord, help me to find in You my only sure refuge.*

BEE'S TONGUE

E KEEP NO stands of bees ourselves, but our flowers are constantly visited by wild ones, especially the plush, fat bumblebees that look like black and yellow chenille.

How long is a bee's tongue? What difference does it make? Plenty. Some varieties of plants, such as clover, would yield little or no seed but for the long-tongued bumblebees that pollinate them. Research has established that the species of bee, the geographical location, the temperature at which the bee is incubated, and the environmental conditions are all factors that affect the length of the bee's tongue.

As for the human tongue, length seems to be an irrelevant matter. Whether long or short, and even though a small member, it is "a fire, a world of iniquity: so is the tongue among our members, that it defileth the whole body, and setteth on fire the course of nature: and it is set on fire of hell" (Jas. 3:6). "Death and life are in the power of the tongue" (Prov. 18:21).

Many a reputation, many a life, has been ruined by a gossip's evil tongue. But many a reputation, many a life, has also been blessed by a kind and good tongue. It might even be said that success or failure on any given day depends on the kind of tongue which has been most intensively employed.

TO THINK ABOUT: *Is my tongue kindling fires, dripping poison, blighting lives?*

TO PRAY ABOUT: *Lord, make my tongue as effective as that of the bee for producing honied sweetness.*

PIT VIPER

ONE DAY I saw a copperhead coiled up at the base of a plum tree. Because of the way its skin pattern joined in that position, it looked like a coil of evenly plaited hair, and was most attractive. The copperhead is about the only poisonous snake we encounter around our place. Like the rattlesnake and eastern moccasin, it is a "pit viper," which is to say that it has a pit between nostril and eye which serves as a thermostat to register heat and cold.

By ingenious experiments it has been ascertained that plugging up these pits deprives the snake of temperature sensations. A snake strikes at a warm light bulb held near an open pit, but makes no move toward one held near a plugged pit. With both pits plugged, the reptile can detect neither heat nor cold.

Some of God's people are about as immobile as a plugged snake: "I know thy works, that thou art neither cold nor hot: I would thou wert cold or hot. So then because thou art lukewarm, and neither cold nor hot, I will spue thee out of my mouth" (Rev. 3:15-16).

Strangely enough, people who cannot stand lukewarm coffee or tepid dishwater are often satisfied to be merely lukewarm Christians. But God knows that a completely cold Christian does less harm to His cause than a lukewarm one, and that only a hot Christian can really register an effective testimony.

To THINK ABOUT: *Do people find me to be hot, lukewarm, or cold in my Christian faith?*

To PRAY ABOUT: *Lord, kindle a fire in my heart that it may burn brightly for You.*

GARBAGE COLLECTOR

EVERY ONCE in a while we lose track of the cattle and have to go in search of them. Sometimes their trail of droppings leads us to them. On one such occasion I watched a lovely little baby-size butterfly flitting along ahead of me. Its wings were a heaven-hued blue with less than an inch spread. It was such a pretty, gay little jewel that my eyes followed its graceful flutter with pleasure.

But my delight turned to disgust when the butterfly lit on a pile of fresh dung, apparently to feed on it. How repulsive it seemed for such a winged beauty, equipped for sunward altitudes, to settle on the earth and feed on filth!

Is such a reversal ever true of God's little ones? Created with wings capable of bearing them Son-ward, are they prone to descend to earth levels and partake of life's refuse? The Holy Spirit commands: "If ye then be risen with Christ, seek those things which are above, where Christ sitteth on the right hand of God. Set your affections on things above, not on things on the earth" (Col. 3:1-2). Let today's diet be manna, not manure.

To THINK ABOUT: *Is my keenest interest and most enthusiastic affection lavished on the filth of this earth?*

To PRAY ABOUT: *Lord, help me to soar Son-ward, toward You.*

HEAVENLY BLUES

AMONG OUR favorite flowers are the heavenly blue morning-glories. We like to plant them along the fences and in places where they will clamber up one tree trunk, then reach over to an adjoining tree or building until the whole yard is festooned with streamers of vine adorned with blossoms of the sky's own blue.

Intriguing about the morning-glory vines are their twisting, spiraling little green tendrils. To me they are a living illustration of faith. They reach out like tiny fingers, lay hold, and then "pull" the vine up. Then they reach out again, take a firm grasp, and "pull" the vine still higher.

That is the way faith acts. However small, it reaches up, lays hold, and what was hope becomes actuality. That is what Hebrews 11:1 says to me: "Faith is the substance of things hoped for, the evidence of things not seen."

The rest of the chapter pictures first one person, then another, putting out the little green tendril of faith under his particular circumstances of misgiving, then laying hold, and through belief in God, pulling himself up to attainment. And remarkable attainments they were, as the entire chapter confirms. With the same little tendrils of faith, holding firmly to the same great God of power, you and I can achieve equally extraordinary things.

To THINK ABOUT: *Am I lying prostrate and dormant because my faith seems small?*

To PRAY ABOUT: *Lord, make me to look not upon my little faith but upon You, the God of power, to whom it clings.*

WALKING STICK

I WENT TO open the screen door and saw a little twig caught in the wire meshes. Only it wasn't a twig after all. It was the insect called a walking stick. Actually, these insects do very little walking, and they hold their two front legs in front of their head so that they look like antennae instead of legs. Certainly they are an excellent example of "protective mimicry," for the casual observer would invariably mistake them for one of the twigs of the small trees on which they live.

Fear of public opinion caused Peter to practice "protective mimicry." Paul says, "When Peter was come to Antioch, I withstood him to the face, because he was to be blamed. For before that certain came from James, he did eat with the Gentiles: but when they were come, he withdrew and separated himself, fearing them which were of the circumcision" (Gal. 2:11-12).

The usefulness of many Christians is impaired when, lacking the courage of their convictions, they fall in with the crowd and conform to their practices. Compromise is the result of cowardice. Daring to be different takes courage. But Christians who stand for something at variance with their environment, for the Lord's sake, retain their testimony and wield their influence for God. Being like God often requires being different from mankind. "Wherefore come ye out from among them, and be ye separate, saith the Lord" (II Cor. 6:17).

To THINK ABOUT: *Whom do I really prefer to resemble: the sinless Son of God or the degenerate sons of Satan?*

To PRAY ABOUT: *Lord, strengthen me that I may refrain from compromise.*

MASKED BANDIT

THE TRELLIS was hung with grapes: lovely, symmetrical, purple clusters that made your mouth water. The next day we would cut the bushel or more that sun, rain, and soil, under God's magic formula, had produced. But when we went out the next morning, not a grape was left on the vines! We knew the culprit.

Raccoons are cute-looking creatures with a band of black fur like a mask across their big, round eyes. They have a button nose, little rounded ears, and paws that leave dainty prints on the lake shore, the hind ones resembling a small child's footprints. But 'coons are bandits and very destructive in their thievery, as the grape incident demonstrated.

To their credit is the habit of washing their food in water before eating it. If this is an indication of their desire for cleanliness, then they are much more particular about what goes into their mouths than many Christians are about what they feed their minds.

"Brethren, whatsoever things are true, whatsoever things are honest, whatsoever things are just, whatsoever things are pure, whatsoever things are lovely, whatsoever things are of good report; if there be any virtue, and if there be any praise, think on these things" (Phil. 4:8). But how can we think on these things and at the same time read or view some of the trashy offerings of modern literature and television?

TO THINK ABOUT: *Are the things I read and the programs I watch honest, pure, lovely, and good?*

TO PRAY ABOUT: *Lord, help me to be as clean about what goes into my mind as about what goes into my mouth.*

115

RACCOONS WASH THEIR FOOD IN WATER

SEPTEMBER

ABOR DAY week end usually climaxes the summer season's hospitality. Work too has tapered off so sometimes we can pack our gear into the car and go fishing. Yes, I mean car, not boat. It sounds ridiculous, doesn't it, to go fishing elsewhere when we have two miles of lake shore of our own? But, you see, there are no rainbow trout in the lake. So we go to one of our state parks where trout are raised and released in the cold, clear, spring-fed streams that gush and rush and twist and tumble their way through scenic beauty. At home, during the same period, we fish for crappie, jack salmon (wall-eyed pike), catfish, or white bass, depending on the temperature, lake height, and muddiness of the water.

This month there are still domestic chores such as canning tomatoes, making wild grape jelly, apple butter, or pear preserves. And there are farm matters such as selling cattle, planting winter pasture, making cattle shelters, fixing fence or gates, spraying, fertilizing, irrigating, and various odd jobs.

In the woods, if it's moist, there are puffball mushrooms a-plenty, and perhaps some other species. The goldenrod and the purple asters complement one another's colors all over the landscape. The sassafras may start donning its coat of many colors as it does every fall ahead of all other shrubs or trees. In the yard, cannas still flaunt their red banners. The zinnias hold stiffly erect their varicolored heads, and the scarlet sage or salvia scatters its bright petals on the ground.

Most of the birds are still with us, feasting on seed. Their courtship songs long ceased, however, it is the eye rather than the ear which must detect their presence. Two exceptions are the whippoorwill and the owl whose night calls give evidence of their unseen activity. Every chipmunk you meet has his jaws puffed out like toothache with the winter supplies he's transporting to his burrow. Fox, squirrel, and even deer are occasionally glimpsed. Tigie dens up a groundhog or rabbit now and then, and lets it be known by her constant excited barking.

Sometimes a neighbor comes down to spend the evening. We invite them to join us in our devotions. Together we relate some of the ways in which God has revealed Himself to us that day.

MORNING DEW

SOME MORNINGS all plant life is wet with dew. Water drips from the "closed shutter" leaf fronds of the mimosa as if it had been deluged with rain. The big suspended spider webs hang so heavy with moisture beads they look as if water could be wrung out of them, if there were anything there to wring. I wish there were some means of weighing or measuring the moisture content of a single web. I think it would be surprising.

In the lowlands the short grass is so dew-pointed it looks as if there has been frost. Wherever the tickle-grass lifts its waterladen lacery of bloom, it looks like a purple haze across the field. Then the sun comes out and in a brief time the dew has evaporated, taking with it all its glamorous witchery.

Much of man's "goodness is as a morning cloud, and as the early dew it goeth away" (Hos. 6:4). On Sunday at services he is good, but on Monday in the office he grasps, schemes, and defrauds. Sick in the hospital he is good, but abroad in the world again, he forgets his vows, and ignores prayer, the Bible, and the church.

Not so with God. "The goodness of God endureth continually" (Ps. 52:1). Yesterday, today, and tomorrow; next week, next year, next century; while time continues, so does God's goodness. Even after time, as man reckons it, has ceased, God's goodness will continue throughout eternity.

TO THINK ABOUT: *Does my goodness regularly evaporate like the early dew?*

TO PRAY ABOUT: *Lord, help me to realize the security that is mine because of Your never-changing, ever-continuing goodness.*

SCARS AND MEDALS

 WAS BURNING some diseased leaf stalks in the incinerator when I accidentally brushed against the wire cover, which left a burn mark across the back of my hand. As I was grooming myself for a dinner party a couple of evenings later, I thought how unsightly the scarred hand would look lifting my water glass and silverware.

Then I remembered another dinner guest with a scar on the hand, one on each palm. It may have been through seeing those scars while He dined with them that the two disciples from Emmaus came to recognize the Lord Jesus Christ. I cringed at the recollection of His hands, nail-scarred for me. People, particularly children, often coax a war veteran to relate how he got his battle scars. Paul explained, "I bear in my body the marks of the Lord Jesus" (Gal. 6:17). He had endured scar-producing physical persecution for Christ's sake.

How rarely do any of us, followers of Christ in this age, display bodily injury for Christ's sake! Few of us bear even an emotional wound for His sake. Is it because we do not feel deeply enough, or witness boldly enough, to engage in battle as soldiers of the cross?

To THINK ABOUT: *If scars for Christ brought medals for courage, would I have any to display?*

To PRAY ABOUT: *Lord, help me to be brave enough to witness wherever and whenever You wish me to.*

BRER FOX

It is only when weather gets severe and other hunting gets slim for him that we have to watch out for Brer Fox in the chicken yard. Given dire enough circumstances, or kill off all his customary prey, and he will invade the domestic precincts and run off with a fowl slung over his shoulder. We've lost ducks that way.

Maybe we'd lose our grapes that way too, if the vines weren't so close to the house, for the Bible says: "Take us the foxes, the little foxes, that spoil the vines: for our vines have tender grapes" (Song of Sol. 2:15).

Grapes in the Scripture are symbolic of the Christian's fruit. Jesus says: "I am the vine, ye are the branches: he that abideth in me, and I in him, the same bringeth forth much fruit: for without me ye can do nothing" (John 15:5).

What "foxes" are spoiling the fruit we would bear for the Master? Not capital sins, such as murder; that would be a "big fox." The despoilers are the "little foxes": procrastination—"I'll do it tomorrow," carelessness—"That'll be good enough for the circle meeting," stinginess—"I can't afford to tithe," unfaithfulness—"I meant to go, but just didn't get around to it," criticism—"If only the preacher wouldn't . . . ," alibis —"I suddenly took a splitting headache," irritability—"If she says that again, I'll scream," oversensitivity—"He never even said thank you," and so on and so on.

To THINK ABOUT: *How negligible can any sin be that spoils the Master's fruit?*

To PRAY ABOUT: *Lord, abide in me and drive out the "little" sins, for without You I can do nothing.*

WE HAVE TO WATCH OUT
FOR BRER FOX

BRUISED WALNUTS

WE HAVE a number of black walnut trees on the farm, and though all do not bear every season, some bear each year. Our best is probably the one a few feet from the kitchen door where it gets irrigation in dry years and is sufficiently accessible to be kept fertilized. Sometimes we fill five or six bushel baskets from this one tree—that is, if the squirrels don't beat us to them.

When we are negligent about keeping them gathered daily as they fall, husks lying on the ground get stepped on and bruised. Split open in this manner, they give off a pungent odor so distinctive I know of nothing to compare it with. Though peculiar, it is quite pleasant and permeates the surrounding air.

The Christian too is supposed to lend fragrance to his surroundings. "Now thanks be unto God which always causeth us to triumph in Christ, and maketh manifest the savour of his knowledge by us in every place. For we are unto God a sweet savour of Christ, in them that are saved, and in them that perish" (II Cor. 2:14-15). Savour means odor or fragrance. To state it simply, God wants us to perfume the world with the sweet fragrance of Christ.

TO THINK ABOUT: *Do I smell like God or like the things of the world?*

TO PRAY ABOUT: *Lord, help me so to affect my surroundings that the fragrance of Christ Himself may really be there where I am.*

122

FOREST PERSONALITIES

It is my ambition to be able to identify every species of tree on our place, but once the leaves are shed, my knowledge falls short. Commonest, of course, are the various oaks, the cedars, sycamore, hickory, walnut, persimmon, basswood, hackberry, redbud, dogwood, and willow.

Sometimes I speculate on which species of tree I would rather be. The oak has so many uses, the dogwood or persimmon but a few. The redbud is very pretty with its heart-shaped leaves and pink flowers, but by legend it is associated with Gethsemane's traitor, so I'd shun being the Judas tree. The walnuts have such beautiful grain, useful for gunstocks, and the wild cherry is prized for furniture.

Such speculation is apparently not unscriptural. The psalmist made this comparison: "I have seen the wicked . . . spreading himself like a green bay tree" (Ps. 37:35).

My conclusion is that I would elect to be a cedar tree—for two reasons. First, the cedar is always green. I want to be that way for the Lord, always giving evidence of growth. Second, the cedar was used in the building of God's temple. I too want to serve in that way. "Ye are the temple of the living God; as God hath said, I will dwell in them, and walk in them: and I will be their God, and they shall be my people" (II Cor. 6:16).

To THINK ABOUT: *In God's economy, how valuable am I—am I useful only for matchsticks or am I stalwart enough for furniture?*

To PRAY ABOUT: *Lord, help me to be a growing Christian, fit building material for use in Your church.*

TRAVELING SEEDS

MOST OF THE summer's blooms have turned to seeds, soon to go globe-trotting. Some will catch a ride on the wind, using their own silk parachutes for this purpose; such are the members of the milkweed family. Some have little hooks for latching onto the fur of passing animals. Others have prongs that enable them to hitchhike rides on people's clothing. Some seeds are water-borne to new places of growth and others are transported by squirrels or birds.

God means for seed to be scattered. "The seed is the word of God" (Luke 8:11). He intends the gospel to be distributed freely and widely: "Ye shall be witness unto me both in Jerusalem, and in all Judea, and in Samaria, and unto the uttermost part of the earth" (Acts 1:8).

Daily, by various methods, every believer ought be scattering the Word: in letters, through tracts and Christian periodicals, in personal conversation and witness, through financing proclamation of the message on television and radio, by giving Bibles as gifts, and by bringing people within earshot of the pulpit. We are not held accountable for the seed's germination, but we are responsible for its distribution.

TO THINK ABOUT: *Have I, in my whole lifetime, distributed as much "seed" as a single milkweed pod?*

TO PRAY ABOUT: *Lord, sow Your seed in me constantly until I witness for You incessantly.*

MUSSEL SHELLS

WHEN THE LAKE goes down, it often exposes the shells of fresh-water mussels. These "clams" as they are sometimes called, form their shells from carbonate of lime extracted from the water. On the outside of this shell is a dull brown membrane which resists the acid in the water and thus protects the iridescent mother-of-pearl lining. The spacing of the concentric lines on this membrane indicates dormant intervals between periods of growth, just as a tree's development is revealed in its growth rings.

What would be demonstrated about our spiritual growth if it were thus recorded? Most Christians show spurts of growth, alternating with periods of dormancy or retardation when there may be no progress for some time. One evidence that growth is taking place is in the Christian skills a person develops. Paul admonished the believers not only to desire these "gifts," but to do so with a proper motive. "Seek that ye may excel to the edifying of the church" (I Cor. 14:12).

To THINK ABOUT: *Is my development and use of God's gifts sporadic, superficial, and self-centered?*

To PRAY ABOUT: *Lord, help me to grow steadily, uniformly, and solely for Your glory and the enrichment of Your church.*

THORN TREES

WE HAVE A FEW of the thorny species of locust trees on our farm, and I'm very careful not to get too close to them. The thorns are so dangerously long and viciously sharp, I am always amazed at how the squirrels can run back and forth on the limbs to get the seed pods without impaling themselves on the thorns.

Once I very gingerly cut enough of the three-inch prongs for each member of my class to have one on the Sunday we studied about the trial and crucifixion of Christ.

"And when they had platted a crown of thorns . . ." (Mat. 27:29). With thorns in hand as we read we realized what it was that He endured for our sins—that painful, gouging crown and all the derision and ignominy that went with it. Handling our thorns carefully lest we prick ourselves and draw blood, we knew too what the Scriptures meant when they said: "Ye have not yet resisted unto blood, striving against sin" (Heb. 12:4).

Our Lord and Savior bled not merely from thorn pricks but from nails and a spear, that we might be redeemed. As His blood trickled away, He paid in full the price of our ransom from sin.

TO THINK ABOUT: *Do I ever sweat, let alone bleed, for Christ, and for victory over sin?*

TO PRAY ABOUT: *Lord, keep me sensitive to what You have suffered for me.*

GLASS BARRIER

As we watch the birds on the feeder trays, we are amused at Pretty Pal, the parakeet. He will fly to the window, alight on the sill and watch their activities too. He does a great deal of twittering in the meanwhile, as if giving a running comment on their appearance and behavior. We suspect that he has a longing to join them but is prevented by that almost invisible pane of glass between him and them.

Sin is what separates man from God. "Your iniquities have separated between you and your God, and your sins have hid his face from you that he will not hear" (Isa. 59:2). Because of that barrier the unbeliever misunderstands Him, misinterprets His message and methods, misses the way to eternal life. Because of the barrier of sin the believer has an impaired fellowship with God, lacking power in prayer and influence in testimony.

In either case, however, there is a way to do away completely with the barrier, by "repentance toward God, and faith toward our Lord Jesus Christ" (Acts 20:21). The unbeliever repents of his rejection of Christ and receives Him as Savior. The believer repents of his trespasses, confesses them to God, and is forgiven and restored to fellowship (cf. I John 1:9). In either case the barrier is eliminated.

To THINK ABOUT: *Have I denied the existence of the barrier because it is not always readily visible?*

To PRAY ABOUT: *Lord, break through whatever separates me from You, that I may be brought to real repentance and true faith.*

HARVEST

HARVEST

ONCE THE CROPS have been harvested, there is opportunity to slow down, to pause and take stock. In retrospect we can inventory the season's products, not alone in tangibles, but also in intangibles; not merely the monetary gains, if such there have been, but more important the sensory dividends. Then we can give thanks for such as these:

For Texture: the serried bristles on a wild turkey's head; the flannel fuzziness of a mullein leaf; the pebbled curve of a hedge apple; the slick smoothness of a peeled willow wand; the fine furriness of a pussy willow catkin . . . .

For Form: the cellular uniformity of a wasp's nursery; the geometrical precision of a spider's web; the decorative spiral of a snail's shell; the radiating symmetry of a mushroom's gills; the circular perfection of a buttonbush ball . . . .

For Motion: the scalloped break of whitecaps on a wave-washed beach; the arched swoop of a belted kingfisher; the trembling nod of breeze-blown leaves; the open and close of a tippling butterfly's wings; the nervous fanning of a fox squirrel's tail; the graceful leap of a fleeing deer . . . .

For Sound: the predawn medley of the music-making mockingbird; the mischievous scamper of inquisitive chipmunks; the rattle and roll of falling acorns; the intermittent staccato of hammering woodpeckers; the liquid melody of the red-winged blackbird; the drowsy monotony of a nocturnal insect's hum; the sleepy twittering of birds disturbed at night; the soft patter of prayed-for raindrops . . . .

For Fragrance: of dew-damp grasses and fog-freshened forests; of a wild plum thicket in frosty bloom; of parasol-protected May-apple blossoms; of wild grape spice wafted on summer winds; of bruised cedar and brookside mint crushed by careless heels . . . .

HARVEST TIME

THERE IS NO more gratifying chore than harvesting. To reach up among the green leaves of a tree and pull off gleaming red apples, or to fill a basket with pink-cheeked, golden pears, gives us great satisfaction. What a pleasure we find it to take clippers and snip tapering purple clusters of grapes from the vine, or to gather pungent nuts from the grass where they nestle at the base of a tree. And the more perfect the fruit or bountiful the yield, the greater our delight. Sometimes, however, the harvest is greater than we can handle. We invite friends to come and pick what they want, but still much of the lovely, luscious fruit must go unharvested.

"The harvest truly is plenteous, but the labourers are few" (Matt. 9:37). In this harvest too, of which Christ speaks, there is the tragedy of too few harvesters. Often there is also too late a concern for the harvest, "The harvest is past, the summer is ended, and we are not saved" (Jer. 8:20).

Both tragedies characterize our Christian life today. Foreign lands once begged for missionaries who would take up residence in their area in order to acquaint them with the gospel and teach them Christ's way of life; but not enough workers were sent, despite their pleas. Now the time seems rapidly to be approaching when there will be no more opportunity for harvest. Unsaved souls will go to their eternal destiny, and we shall be blameworthy for their lost condition because we failed to get concerned about it in time.

To THINK ABOUT: *Am I neglecting a "plenteous harvest" next door, at school or office, in club or class?*

To PRAY ABOUT: *Lord, make me willing and ready to go reaping before it is too late.*

GREEN PERSIMMONS

ONE OF the pretties of fall are the persimmons with their bluish bloom over the red-brown of the skin of the fruit. These little fruits are a crop that seems never to fail. Although they are not as juicy and luscious in drouth years as in moist ones, their very presence is a boon to wild life whose other forms of provender may be lacking. Deer, 'coons, squirrels, almost all of the animals eat them. Humans do too. We make a pudding of them which our guests term "out of this world."

If you want to play a really "ornery" joke on someone, you can inveigle him into eating an underripe persimmon. It contains an extraordinarily astringent element which makes your mouth and lips feel as if they were turned inside out. So vivid is this sensation of reverseness that you wonder if they will ever really return to normal.

When lips are not used in the praise and blessing for which God purposed them, they really are in reverse. "Put away from thee a froward mouth, and perverse lips put far from thee" (Prov. 4:24). "Better is the poor that walketh in his integrity, than he that is perverse in his lips" (Prov. 19:1). God can make no use of green persimmon lips.

To THINK ABOUT: *How can I use my lips to brighten and bless someone's life today?*

To PRAY ABOUT: *Lord, open my lips that my mouth may show forth Your praise.*

MONARCH BUTTERFLY

Because a killing frost was predicted, we picked all the dahlias, and we had some gorgeous ones. I placed them in a vase on the sun porch which, though unheated, we thought would be above freezing. Next morning we found that some of them had been damaged by frigid temperature. On one of them we found a tawny-winged Monarch butterfly. When we brought it into a warm room it revived, but apparently its nerve centers had been damaged because it would zoom up and bump into things or else wing an erratic course in an unbalanced fashion.

I fixed a little vessel of sugar water, and whenever I set the butterfly on its brim, it would unroll the long tongue it had curled up under its chin and sip the man-made nectar. I set it on one of the potted plants in our greenhouse window, and it flew about a bit, then flopped helplessly into a corner and lay there until I came to its rescue. It was there that I eventually found it, dead, perhaps due to my failure to have picked it up again and brought it to the sugar water for nourishment.

When sin has paralyzed a man's conscience until he can no longer make his way alone toward Christ, spiritual death is all that awaits him. "The man that wandereth out of the way of understanding shall remain in the congregation of the dead" (Prov. 21:16). Sometimes, though, another can help him find his way back to the springs of living water.

To think about: *Has my cold unconcern allowed an acquaintance to drift erratically into spiritual death?*

To pray about: *Lord, use me to restore some helpless soul to Your way.*

FLYAWAY PARAKEET

WHEN THE door was opened, out swooped Pretty Pal the parakeet, into the vast and windswept landscape of autumn. All day he flew to and fro, either in the tops of the tall oaks or in the more lowly peach and mimosa branches. Sometimes he circled as redheaded woodpeckers rudely pursued him. But he would not respond to our invitation to return to his own residence. Dusk and chill of night came on. It began to rain and the temperature dropped. We grieved for Pretty Pal, thinking he was most likely lost, wet, and cold. We assumed he would not survive the near-freezing temperature.

To our surprise and joy, daylight revealed him again flitting among the trees, so we hung his cage on the clothesline. Presently we saw him in it, and soon he was coming and going. When nightfall came, we brought him in, but later we again hung the cage outside with its door open. Pretty Pal left it, but after being chased by starlings and woodpeckers he returned to it and thereafter showed no desire to leave it. Perhaps he had learned that a cage was intended not only to keep him in but also to keep harm out.

Most people go a lifetime without realizing that this is the ultimate purpose of God's restrictions. His "Thou shalt not" is not intended simply to restrain us and curtail our freedom or enjoyment. It is also a safeguard to protect us and assure our best welfare. The commands of the Bible all reveal this fact: "The paths of the Lord are mercy and truth unto such as keep his covenant and his testimonies" (Ps. 25:10).

TO THINK ABOUT: *Have I been mistaking God's stockades for prisons, His safeguards for shackles?*

TO PRAY ABOUT: *Lord, help me to see mercy and truth in Your commandments.*

SCATTERED SHOWERS

NOT INFREQUENTLY on a fall day the weatherman predicts "scattered showers." Sometimes we can actually see such a weather pattern. Low-hanging clouds and a streaked horizon across the lake disclose that it is raining over there, though not around us. At other times we are in the midst of falling rain while in the distance we can see the sun brightly shining. Most people attribute such climatic vagaries to differing topography, air channels, or other factors.

But the Bible indicates God may be using the weather for special purposes. "I caused it to rain upon one city and caused it not to rain upon another city: one piece was rained upon, and the piece whereupon it rained not withered" (Amos 4:7).

This passage and its context indicate that God was seeking to draw His people to repentance. Numerous Bible passages indicate that drought and flood, blasting and mildew, hail, and other weather conditions are sometimes employed by God for disciplinary purposes. Therefore it is ours to inquire after their significance in our own lives.

Weather conditions are not the only means God uses to bring people to repentance, but whatever the nature of His means, the purpose back of it is begotten of love, of God's desire for our best welfare. "Despisest thou the riches of his goodness and forbearance and longsuffering; not knowing that the goodness of God leadeth thee to repentance?" (Rom. 2:4).

TO THINK ABOUT: *Is God seeking to reason with me today through the weather?*

TO PRAY ABOUT: *Lord, help me at all times to have a heart sensitive to that goodness which leads to repentance.*

SUSPENDED ANIMATION

ONE OF the most annoying and destructive creatures around the farm is the groundhog or woodchuck. This ungainly rodent with shaggy brownish-black fur is a great burrower. Because of his need for numerous escape ways from his den, he'll tunnel up an entire hillside with open holes which are a hazard to livestock as well as to men. He subsists on grasses, vegetables, and fruit, and is really a hog about it. Consequently he puts on a deal of weight, particularly as it comes time for him to hibernate.

As early as October in some sections of the country, he retreats to his burrow where he remains in a state of suspended animation until spring, drawing on the layers of fat for sustenance. On February 2, according to tradition, he emerges to look for his lean, lank shadow in the sun. If he sees it, he returns to his den for six more weeks.

Many a Christian might as well be in hibernation, so far as his spiritual value to church and community is concerned. He withdraws into a state of suspended animation of the soul, and tries to exist on the stored-up spiritual experiences of long ago. Daily spiritual food and exercise are essential to robust Christian growth, as is evidenced by Luke's account of the Bereans who "received the word with all readiness of mind, and searched the scriptures daily, whether those things were so" (Acts 17: 11), and of other believers who "daily in the temple, and in every house, . . . ceased not to teach and preach Jesus Christ" (Acts 5:42).

To THINK ABOUT: *Have I ceased studying God's Word and witnessing to His work, thus going into spiritual hibernation?*

To PRAY ABOUT: *Lord, goad me, if need be, out of my selfish burrow of inactivity into fruitful service.*

140

SIGNATURE SPIDER

WHILE I was making the bed I discovered a "signature" spider and its web on the window screen. The insect was a handsome lady with a black body about an inch long on which were lemon yellow markings. Its long, velvety legs were orange where they joined the body. It was resting head-down in the center of the trapezoid web on a zigzag band of silk which reminded me of the factory mends I've seen on certain knit rayon garments sold as seconds. This white band of silk is the final touch in weaving the web as if "finis" were being written. That is why it is called the signature spider.

After spinning a brown parchment-like cocoon about the size of a hickory nut and fastening it to the window screen, the spider had deposited a mass of eggs in it. Then her lifework was done.

Any hour, any day, for any of us, without forewarning, "finis" may be written over our lifework. Do we want the record to stand the way it is at this moment? Are we ready to affix our signature mindful of the fact that "every one of us shall give account of himself to God" (Rom. 14:12)? Are we ready to "appear before the judgment seat of Christ; that every one may receive the things done in his body, according to that he hath done, whether it be good or bad" (II Cor. 5:10)?

To THINK ABOUT: *Am I prepared now to render my account to the Righteous Judge?*

To PRAY ABOUT: *Spare me, good Lord; reward me not according to my iniquities.*

NOVEMBER

In our state, squirrel, quail, waterfowl, rabbit, and deer are all legal game this month. But deer hunting is what stirs up the excitement. One of the first symptoms of the deer fever epidemic is the rash of red caps. About every male in the population appears in one, whether he is actually a hunter, or is merely in danger of being mistaken for the hunted. Men are seen in the sports shops fingering high-powered rifles. Some travel miles to locate a legal firearm that can be borrowed or rented.

Walk up to any ring of sidewalk pedestrians and you're almost certain to hear remarks like, "I'm hunting on my wife's uncle's brother-in-law's place," or "I've spotted a deer run down by the bridge and aim to set up my stand there," or "I've built a blind out in my pasture."

Stick around long enough and you'll hear a real yarn: about the fellow who was almost stampeded by an eight-pointer, and had buck fever so bad he couldn't pull the trigger, or about the farmer who had to watch one browse all day without shooting it, because it was just across the fence on his neighbor's land.

Included in the gabble will be accounts of the abnormals, like the doe with only three legs who had a pair of fawn following her, or the white albino all had agreed not to shoot, but which some "outsider" killed. There will be gossip about the hunters who got lost or wet—or caught! In the last category will be those who triggered too early or too late, or the hoggish ones who weren't satisfied with a single kill.

Some of the hunters regard the passive hours spent on a stand waiting for game to come their way as time filched from life's hubbub for communing with God and musing on His mercies.

SUNLIGHT SEEKERS

DEER HUNTERS always make their way to their stations before dawn so as not to be observed moving around after daylight. One who had thus watched the sunrise made an interesting observation. As it began to get light the birds began to flit about, but the places where they lit were in the treetops which were gilded by the sunlight; on other trees, or lower down on the same tree where shadows prevailed, there were no birds—invariably they chose the sunlit treetops.

Christ told His people to frequent the sunlight too: "While ye have the light, believe in the light, that ye may be the children of light" (John 12:36). Of course He was referring to *Son*light. He also observed that "he that doeth truth cometh to the light, that his deeds may be made manifest, that they are wrought in God" (John 3:21).

With Christ as the light of the world, everyone has a source of light to which he may turn. If his heart is right through its confidence in that light, he will have no desire to seek the shadow. He will have no fear of being scrutinized in that light. It is only the one who is guilty who fears God and wants to remain unobserved in the shadowy areas of life.

TO THINK ABOUT: *Do I shun the light that streams from God's Word and find excuses for avoiding it?*

TO PRAY ABOUT: *Lord, stir me to seek light from You each day anew.*

SCARED CAT

LITTLE KITTY was fond of her master. She often followed him to the feed house and barn and even up the hill to the far barn. Then she took to following him to the duck blind. While he waited there in the cold, she'd rub against his legs and purr. He might even have to give her a rude push when he hastily raised his sights and took aim. But once the gun had been fired little kitty was no longer to be seen. The blast dissipated all her loyalty. She shot out of that blind as fast as any bullet, for she wasn't there for action, but only as a pastime.

No Christian knows the enormity of his cowardice or the puniness of his courage until a real test comes. Paul reported that at his first trial no man stood by him; they all forsook him, just as the disciples all forsook Christ at His trial. How was it that big blustery Peter was cowed by a slip of a girl while little boy David never quailed before the mighty giant? What made the difference?

"Not by might, nor by power, but by my spirit, saith the Lord of hosts" (Zech. 4:6). Only as we "take the helmet of salvation, and the sword of the spirit, which is the word of God" can we "be strong in the Lord and in the power of his might" (Eph. 6:17, 10). Otherwise we too, with the disciples, will absent ourselves like a scared cat at the critical moment.

To THINK ABOUT: *At what point does my loyalty to Christ vanish?*

To PRAY ABOUT: *Lord, grant me the Spirit who will keep me close to You and make me willing, if necessary, to suffer shame or pain for Your sake.*

STORED BULBS

FTER THE first killing frost has laid low the foliage, our flower bulbs must be lifted from the ground and laid out in the basement to dry. When this has been accomplished, they are boxed in sand or sawdust to await the coming of spring. But this rest period is not a matter of wasted time. I have noticed that, whether I unpot it or not, if I do not set the amaryllis aside for a few weeks it does not bloom the next period.

Christians need rest periods too in order to store up reserves from which to put forth bloom and subsequently bear spiritual fruit. Jesus said to the disciples, "Come ye yourselves apart into a desert place, and rest a while" (Mark 6:31). But rest does not mean indolence or indifference, it means a deliberate program that will renew and revitalize. Lots of God's people do need just plain sleep, but the hour of the worship service is not the time for that. Worship can be the very dynamo needed to restore spiritual reserves.

In fact, this was the purpose for which God ordained a weekly day set apart for Him. To be sure, Christ said that "the sabbath was made for man" (Mark 2:27). But He ordained that Christian fellowship—sermon and song, not just sleep—be a part of it: "Not forsaking the assembling of ourselves together, as the manner of some is" (Heb. 10:25). There is no substitute for public worship from the standpoint either of obedience to God or of values to be derived from it.

TO THINK ABOUT: *Have I been substituting lazy inactivity for constructive restoration?*

TO PRAY ABOUT: *Lord, help me to value and exercise the blessed privilege of regular public worship.*

BURIED CANES

URYING THE rose and raspberry canes is a dismal task, but a very important one. Were it not done, the shrubs would, with any warm spell, sprout and start to grow out of season. Then they would be damaged the first time it turned cold. To bury them from sight, however, does seem at first glance like an act of severance and a termination of all that is lovely and promising.

And so it seems when the body of a loved one must be interred. Yet if the deceased has known Christ in the full pardon of sin and has been reborn spiritually through faith in His atonement, there is no more cause for despair than in burying the rose canes. Both will bloom again.

That is what Christ was telling Mary and Martha: "Thy brother shall rise again . . . I am the resurrection, and the life: he that believeth in me, though he were dead, yet shall he live" (John 11:23, 25). Paul explained the matter in these words: "If in this life only we have hope in Christ, we are of all men most miserable. But now is Christ risen from the dead and become the firstfruits of them that slept . . . for as in Adam all die, so in Christ shall all be made alive" (I Cor. 15:19–20, 22). The loved ones from whom we are separated for a time will be reunited with us when, in Christ, we all are made alive.

TO THINK ABOUT: *Have I been viewing death as a terminal at the end of life instead of as a tunnel into the life eternal?*

TO PRAY ABOUT: *"Thanks be to God, who giveth us the victory through our Lord Jesus Christ."*

FERTILITY CYCLE

THE HAULING and spreading of manure plays a role in one of God's remarkable modes of operation: manure fertilizes the soil, which causes vegetation to thrive, which in turn is devoured and digested by the cattle and transformed either into butterfat and beef or into a residue which is returned to the ground once more as fertilizer.

There is no waste in God's economy, no surplus commodities, no obsolete items. After feeding the thousands, Christ commanded that the unused portions be gathered in order that nothing be lost.

If a person is in the circle of God's will, there is a place of service for him. None need feel unnecessary or in the way, or that he has outlived his usefulness. "Now are they many members, yet but one body . . . Nay, much more those members of the body, which seem to be more feeble, are necessary" (Cor. 12:20, 22).

God has a use for each of us as long as He leaves us here on earth. Our part is to seek to know His purpose for us and adjust to it, whatever it is, without complaint or criticism.

To THINK ABOUT: *Have I co-operated with God in the part He planned for me in His universal cycle of utility?*

To PRAY ABOUT: *Lord, lead me to a full awareness of Your purpose for my life and enable me to achieve the usefulness You desire of me.*

FOOTPRINTS

WHENEVER THERE is heavy rain or snow, we find the tracks of wild life in our fields, through the woods, and along the lake. Their location, as well as the actual imprint, help to identify their maker. If they persistently border the lake, they are apt to belong to a raccoon. If they lead from brush pile to brush pile, they may be those of a rabbit.

A Christian's footprints should always follow a prescribed course. "Hereunto were ye called; because Christ also suffered for us, leaving us an example, that ye should follow his steps" (I Pet. 2:21). The trouble is that not many of us want to follow His trail of suffering; we prefer instead the path of ease or luxury.

"Unto you it is given in the behalf of Christ not only to believe on him, but also to suffer for his sake" (Phil. 1:29). It is hard to reckon suffering as a gift, as much a gift as faith itself. Yet if we will accept it in that light, and pray for His purposes to be accomplished through it, we can benefit by it, and fulfil our calling.

To THINK ABOUT: *Have I been rating myself above my Lord in thinking I should be exempt from pain?*

To PRAY ABOUT: *Lord, enable me to accept suffering with You as readily as I do Your redemption.*

WE FIND THE TRACKS OF
WILD LIFE THROUGH THE WOODS

LOOKING BACK

TIGIE LOVES to ride to the mailbox in the truck and then hotfoot it back. Part of the way she has her own short cuts which take her from view. But part of the way her course parallels the road, so we can see the steady speed that usually enables her to beat us back to the garage.

During stormy weather one evening she was racing over the icy snow when she looked back to make sure that she was in the lead. In that split second she lost her footing and went tobogganing down a slippery hill in comical fashion. I don't know whether the experience taught her the hazards of looking back or not.

Lot's wife is notorious for that mistake. Christ warned against it. He declared, "No man, having put his hand to the plow, and looking back, is fit for the kingdom of God" (Luke 9:62). The plowman can't turn a straight furrow if he's looking back over his shoulder. The resultant crop, crowded in spots, will be less productive.

To plow a straight furrow the operator must have his eye focused ahead on some distant point. The Christian's eye is to be on Jesus: "Looking unto Jesus the author and finisher of our faith" (Heb. 12:2). Water does not afford very secure footing for a stroll; yet Peter managed to walk even on the surface of the lake—until he took his eyes off of Jesus. In that moment he began to waver and sink. Whenever we fail to look ahead—unto Jesus—our footsteps will falter.

To THINK ABOUT: *Have I been looking back to the Christ-less days of my life to find direction, standards, and strength?*

To PRAY ABOUT: *Lord, help me to keep my eyes upon You at all times, and draw me, through faith, into Your kingdom.*

UNUSED WINGS

IT WAS a late fall day with a light snow on the ground. I had chosen to enjoy it to the utmost by a walk through the woods. As I trod softly down an old abandoned road which wound along beside one of our fences, I heard a quick, nervous movement in the fallen leaves on the ground. I "froze" and searched the landscape.

On down the lane fifty to hundred feet from me, and on the other side of the fence, was a wild turkey hen. She was running to and fro, agitatedly seeking a way through. The fence was woven wire about eighteen inches high, and topped by a couple of strands of barbed wire. She would trot along it, poking her head through the wire mesh every now and then, then change direction and make the same vain effort coming back. Over and over she repeated her frustrating circuit.

Now a wild turkey is capable of high and lengthy flight. So I wondered, as I watched her vainly trying to get *through* the fence: why doesn't she use her wings and fly *over* it?

Her frantic action was really quite human. God has promised that "They that wait upon the Lord shall renew their strength: they shall mount up with wings as eagles" (Isa. 40:31). Yet more often than not, we followers of His behave just like the wild turkey hen. We beat our heads helplessly against the problems and obstacles that confront us, never even developing—much less using—the strength that comes from Him.

TO THINK ABOUT: *Am I using God's provision for victory?*

TO PRAY ABOUT: *Lord, strengthen the wings of my faith so that I shall rise above difficulties.*

GATHERING EGGS

IN GATHERING the eggs, we occasionally come upon a soft shell or a peculiarly pointed or pebbled one; but mostly our hens lay great big eggs of superior quality. Saturday's gathering is always set aside to take to our pastor as a sort of tithe, for the Scripture says: "Thou shalt truly tithe all of the increase of thy seed that the field bringeth forth year by year" (Deut. 14:22).

We also give our pastor a tenth of the fryers we raise for our own use each year, and other first fruits from time to time. This does not take the place of the monetary tithe of all cash income we receive. Over the years we have experienced the promised blessing: "Bring ye all the tithes into the storehouse, that there may be meat in mine house, and prove me now herewith, saith the Lord of hosts, if I will not open you the windows of heaven, and pour you out a blessing, that there shall not be room enough to receive it" (Mal. 3:10).

This does not mean that we are legalistic, fraction-figuring tithers. Being under grace changes our motivation. We no longer want to escape the tithe but to exceed it. "You can give without loving, but you can't love without giving." God does so much for us we can't possibly do enough for Him.

To THINK ABOUT: *Is my love the kind that rejoices over opportunities to share?*

To PRAY ABOUT: *Lord, deliver me from the covetousness which would close my hands instead of opening them.*

DECEMBER

WE ALWAYS decorate for Christmas, even though, due to inclement weather, we are sometimes the only ones to see our decorations. Moreover, on the assumption that there will be visitors, we prepare an extra supply of pies, cakes, cookies, pudding, and particularly candies. We even provide special treats for the livestock, pets, and wild life.

Then there are the packages to wrap and dispatch. And the letter writing never gets finished: rather than send out cards, we write personal notes. We begin at Thanksgiving with the intent of having it done before the holiday rush, but invariably we find ourselves in correspondence clear up to New Year's Day.

At this season there are always extra programs and meetings to attend, while social affairs multiply and offer a special warmth and sparkle appropriate to the season. The remembrances are fun too, coming as they do from far and wide. One of my favorites, without which it wouldn't be Christmas, is a blooming poinsettia, the Lord's own way of showing how vivid red can be.

Throughout the month there are constant reminders, if one has his heart open to them, of the marvelous God who planned the first Christmas and provided the Supreme Gift. Despite the crowded days and the rushing hours, if we will we can contemplate the tokens of God's love and lift our hearts to Him in appreciation.

SWIMMING TURKEY

THE OTHER day a flock of wild turkeys came flying across the arm of the lake, a distance of perhaps a quarter of a mile. They landed right in the front yard so there was no mistaking them. For some reason, one hen didn't make it clear across. She lit on the water about seventy-five feet from the bank. I watched her through the binoculars, expecting to see her sink. Instead, her movements indicated her feet and legs were paddling up and down in a swimming stroke. Her long tail feathers streaming out behind her no doubt gave her buoyancy and balance. As I watched, she climbed up on the bank, shook herself like a dog, and joined the other turkeys foraging in the yard.

God helps His children too when they get caught beyond their depth. "When thou passest through the waters, I will be with thee; and through the rivers, they shall not overflow thee" (Isa. 43:2). Water here symbolizes trials. God will not let the waves of affliction pass over our heads and submerge us. "God is faithful, who will not suffer you to be tempted above that ye are able; but will with the temptation also make a way to escape, that ye may be able to bear it" (I Cor. 10:13).

To THINK ABOUT: *Have I appreciated the faithfulness of Him who guards my life?*

To PRAY ABOUT: *Lead me not into temptation but deliver me from evil, O God of my salvation.*

BROKEN BOUGHS

SOME TREES are badly broken by ice storms while others remain undamaged. Location is not what makes the difference, for they may be standing side by side. Under those circumstances, in a given storm, it cannot be the amount of the load either.

There is but one explanation: the nature of the wood. That is why our American elm remains unscathed while the Chinese elm becomes a shambles of broken limbs. The branches of the former bend under the ice's weight; those of the latter have no "give" and consequently break.

Human nature reacts similarly to the stresses of life. One individual has a breakdown, whereas another in practically the same situation buckles down and draws dividends on his difficulties. What determines a man's "tensile strength"? Is it his inherited constitution, his environment, his training? It may very well be none of these, but rather his relationship to God.

Through faith in Christ a man actually has supernatural resources. "I can do all things through Christ which strengtheneth me" (Phil. 4:13). Paul's confidence may be ours too. Drawing on His reserves we can meet our tensions with equanimity and be made better, not bitter, by them.

To THINK ABOUT: *Have my stresses resulted in gripes or growth?*

To PRAY ABOUT: *Lord, show me how to capitalize on my conflicts.*

PAMPERED PETS

ON A winter night when the wind is howling and the temperature low, and we are snug and well fed ourselves, it is a satisfaction to know that our cattle, poultry, and pets are equally well cared for. To provide for them thus is in keeping with Scripture: "A righteous man regardeth the life of his beast" (Prov. 12:10). No practice, however, or proverb either can justify putting a dog before God. When that is done, more than mere spelling has been reversed.

Nevertheless, statistics indicate that financially many persons do put their creatures before their Creator. Americans spend three billion dollars a year on their pets, two to three million of this sum going for dog food alone. We blush with shame to compare that figure with what they give their God.

"Thou shalt have no other gods before me" (Exod. 20:3). Anything in our lives which takes priority over God, no matter what it is, has become for us an idol, and has usurped the place which He alone should have. How must it make God feel when we show more devotion to an animal than to Him?

TO THINK ABOUT: *Would I want my loved ones to be as unmindful of me as I am of God?*

TO PRAY ABOUT: *Lord, forgive my failure to give You the pre-eminence in my life.*

DUCKS AT OUR DOOR

At times there are hundreds of mallard ducks visiting in our vicinity. Once they had been swimming in the waters quite close to our house, but as cold weather continued and ice formed on our cove, their gathering place became more and more distant. I began praying the Lord to melt the ice; I hoped that would bring them back to our area.

Instead of growing warmer and thawing, it remained cold, and more snow fell, making the lake resemble a snow-covered plain. We could still see the ducks dimly on the distant channel, which had not frozen over. One afternoon I glanced out the window and saw birds flying our way. To my delight about twenty ducks lit on the snow-covered ice of the lake about a hundred yards across the cove. They began waddling toward the bank where quantities of smartweed seed were to be found. Others followed, and presently there were hundreds of them swarming over the bank like bees on a honeycomb.

Then and there God spoke to my heart, showing me that though He had not granted my specific petition (He had not thawed the ice on the lake), He had answered my prayer and given me my true desire: a closer view of the ducks. "The Lord God is a sun and shield: the Lord will give grace and glory: no good thing will he withhold from them that walk uprightly" (Ps. 84:11).

To THINK ABOUT: *Have I discounted the power of prayer because my specific petitions were not always granted?*

To PRAY ABOUT: *Lord, help me to realize that You always hear, even when You do not answer in the way I expect.*

"FLOATING" DEER

*I*T WAS when I was taking Christmas mail to the box that I saw a fleet white-tailed buck start across the road in front of me. He ran a few feet and then "froze," giving me opportunity to admire his trim beige body, his soft brown eyes, and his sensitive, sniffing nostrils. Then, catching my scent, he quickly took off. He seemed to rise without effort and gracefully "float" over a near-by fence, his white tail a farewell blur like a fleecy cloud on a distant horizon.

How could he leap over obstructions with such apparent ease? I wished I were able to overcome the obstacles in my path as successfully. How could I sail over all the hustle of holiday activity that was pushing and crowding me until I was cross and worn?

"Martha, Martha, thou art careful and troubled about many things: But one thing is needful" (Luke 10:41). There was my mistake, the cause of my earthboundness! I had lost sight of Christ and the honor due Him. No wonder I couldn't soar. No wonder I was fenced in with fret and fatigue. If I'd elevate Christ to His proper place and subordinate the other aspects of Christmas to the lower plane where they belonged, I'd surmount my difficulties and regain my poise, and with it my strength. "In quietness and in confidence shall be your strength" (Isa. 30:15).

To THINK ABOUT: *Am I exhausting myself in the holiday activities that crowd Christ out of Christmas?*

To PRAY ABOUT: *Lord, bring me by Your strength to a quiet confidence in the one thing needful.*

I SAW A FLEET WHITE-TAILED BUCK

CHRISTMAS DECORATIONS

WE SOMETIMES make our own Christmas decorations. I gather sycamore balls while they are green enough to forestall disintegration. Then I paint them bright colors, or silver or gild them. I cement glittering sequins onto the velvety green leaves of a mullein head. That produces glamour in unusual fashion. Little weed stalks are immersed in thin starch and then dipped into artificial snow. Also we string colored lights on the cedar outside the door, and have a living Christmas tree. The jays and cardinals help out by perching on the green limbs like animated ornaments.

God wants Christians to be animated ornaments too, "shewing all good fidelity; that they may adorn the doctrine of God our Saviour in all things" (Titus 2:10). How remarkable that we may actually *adorn* or decorate His teaching.

Our fidelity or constancy is the key to this adornment. Think of all the Christian virtues in which constancy may conceivably be shown: love, kindness, sympathy, generosity, reliability, truthfulness, purity, to name but a few. Think too of what dull adornment they make if manifested only spasmodically, waveringly, or occasionally. "Therefore . . . be ye stedfast, unmoveable, always abounding in the work of the Lord, forasmuch as ye know that your labour is not in vain in the Lord" (I Cor. 15:58).

To THINK ABOUT: *Is my Christian constancy of such a kind as to adorn the doctrine of Christ?*

To PRAY ABOUT: *Lord, help me to be a consistently loyal disciple.*

SELECTING A TREE

WE WENT to the woods to select a cedar for our Christmas tree. There was no lack of them. There were those so tall their tips would have touched the ceiling, and those so tiny they would have been suitable for a doll's house. There were squat, bushy ones and stately, thin ones. But seek as we would, we could never find one that was just right. Some had bare spots where limbs had failed to grow. On others the limbs were thicker or longer on one side than on the other. Still others were not erect, but crooked; or they were not an attractive shade of green. All were deficient in some respect.

People lack symmetry and balance too. Even Christians vary in stature and hue. One is long on prayer, but short on patience. Another is strong on worship but weak on giving. Still others are thick in flattery but lean on gratitude.

The scriptural standard is a uniformity of development: "Speaking the truth in love . . . grow up unto him in all things" (Eph. 4:15). All things, it says, not just a few, or some things.

God intends for every believer well-rounded Christian growth: "That in everything ye are enriched by him . . . so that ye come behind in no gift" (I Cor. 1:5, 7). Any deficiency of Christian development is due, not to His failure to provide, but to our failure to appropriate.

To THINK ABOUT: *In what respect am I a lopsided Christian?*

To PRAY ABOUT: *Lord, enrich me with every needful gift that in all things I may grow up unto You.*

SNOW-LADEN TREES

A WET SNOW was falling. In a brief time there was a thick layer on the ground, and a heavy accumulation on the trees. As we looked out the window from time to time we saw their branches bending lower and lower from the weight of the flaky white stuff. Then it ceased falling and in a surprisingly short time the wind was shifting to the south and the sun was shining. Before long the snow began to melt.

As it did, I noticed the tree limbs springing back into place. They were no longer bent almost to the ground. Had they been capable of human emotions and words, they might have exclaimed, "What a relief! How wonderful to be rid of that burden!"

People sometimes get "bent over" with the weight of their cares and problems. They begin to sag spiritually and are soon "touching bottom" as if they had no God, no assurance, and no hope. They are guilty of disobedience. They have failed in "casting all your care upon him; for he careth for you" (I Pet. 5:7).

God either lightens the burden or strengthens the back. Either the snow will melt, permitting the branch to spring back up; or the branch will arch, supporting the weight imposed upon it. In either event, God is mindful of the weight. He cares.

TO THINK ABOUT: *Am I willing to trust God to lift the burden when it is His appointed time?*

TO PRAY ABOUT: *Lord, grant me grace to "arch" triumphantly under my burdens and accept them as blessings from You.*

163

THEIR BRANCHES WERE BENDING
LOWER AND LOWER

MASTER'S RETURN

TIGIE IS JUST an ordinary, shaggy little black and brown dog who likes to be with her master. If he drives the truck, she wants to sit at his side. If he leaves in the boat, she is sure to be along. If he works in the shop, she is lying close by. Just to be near him makes her a happy little dog.

She does not go with him to tend the cattle, however. She goes instead to the head of the path by which he will return, and there she waits and watches. She sits alertly —head cocked, ears upright, nose sniffing, eyes scanning the landscape—ready at any moment to rejoice in a reunion with the one she loves.

At Jesus' ascension, an angel told the disciples: "Ye men of Galilee, why stand ye gazing up into heaven? This same Jesus, which is taken up from you into heaven, shall so come in like manner as ye have seen him go into heaven" (Acts 1:11). Paul firmly believed this: "The Lord himself shall descend from heaven with a shout, with the voice of the archangel, and with the trump of God: and the dead in Christ shall rise first: then we which are alive and remain shall be caught up together with them in the clouds, to meet the Lord in the air: and so shall we ever be with the Lord" (I Thess. 4:16-17). Christians must and do expect Christ's return at any time.

Until then, I hope I can love the thought of His appearing and, like faithful Tigie, alertly anticipate my Master's coming. I hope He finds me watching as patiently, and eagerly!

"Even so, come, Lord Jesus."